the Wild Butcher
From Field to Table

by the Editors at
Creative Publishing international

Creative Publishing
international

www.creativepub.com

Creative Publishing
international

Copyright © 2007 by Creative Publishing international, Inc.
18705 Lake Drive East
Chanhassen, MN 55317
1-800-328-3895
www.creativepub.com
All rights reserved.

Printed in China
10 9 8 7 6 5 4 3 2 1

Library of Congress Cataloging-in-Publication Data

The wild butcher : from field to table / by the editors at
Creative Publishing international.
    p. cm.
Includes index.
  ISBN-13: 978-1-58923-319-5 (soft cover)
  ISBN-10: 1-58923-319-0 (soft cover)
 1. Game and game-birds, Dressing of. 2. Cookery (Game)
I. Creative Publishing International. II. Title.

 SK283.8W55 2007
 799.2'4—dc22   2006029239

THE WILD BUTCHER
by the Editors at Creative Publishing
international, Inc.

President/CEO: Ken Fund
Vice President Sales/Marketing: Peter Ackroyd
Publisher: Winnie Prentiss
Executive Managing Editor: Barbara Harold
Book Designer: Deb Pierce
Production Managers: Laura Hokkanen, Linda Halls

Creative Director: Michele Lanci-Altomare
Senior Design Manager: Brad Springer
Design Managers: Jon Simpson, Mary Rohl
Book Designer: Deb Pierce

the Wild
Butcher

Contents

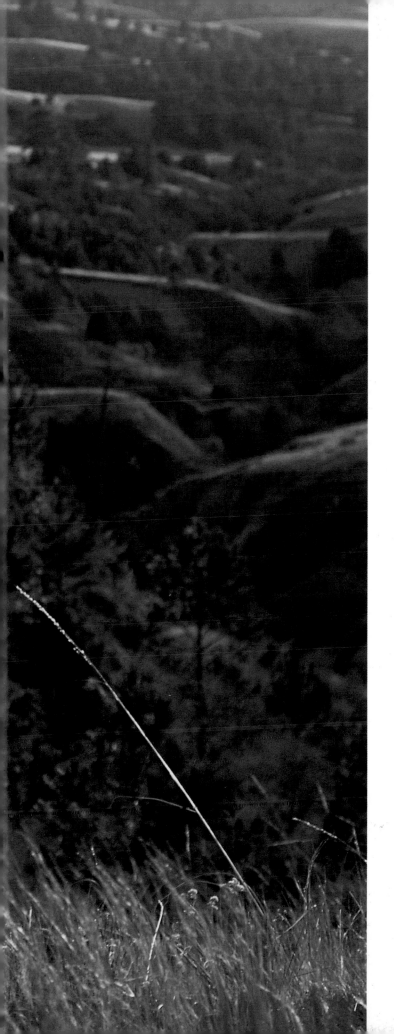

Preparing Wild Game

Great-tasting wild game dishes begin long before the meat ever touches a frying pan. Good cooking begins in the field with a good shot, proper care and attention to detail. The real work begins once the animal is on the ground. The work can at times be a bit messy, but proper game care and field dressing are essential to preserving the quality of the meat. Study the illustrated directions presented here so that you learn to properly care for downed birds, big-game and small-game animals. There are no second chances to turn a recently bagged wild animal into top-notch table fare. Take your time and do it right.

The next step is efficient butchering, wrapping and freezing. The correct cutting and wrapping of meat will ensure you top quality and delicious cuts of meat for many months to come. The step-by-step instructions shown here are easy to follow, and with practice your results will look just as good as those appearing on these pages. There are very few shortcuts in the preservation of game meat. All the hard work you put into planning your hunt, field dressing and caring for your game will be for nothing if you fail to preserve the meat properly. It is much more important that you finish the step correctly instead of just quickly.

When it comes time to eat, there is nothing better than properly prepared wild game. The meat is low in fat, high in protein and exceptionally flavorful. The recipes run the gamut from the gourmet table to the picnic bench, and each one offers a unique opportunity for you to complete the circle by harvesting, preparing, preserving, cooking and, finally, enjoying your game at the table.

Big Game: Field Dressing & Transport

A little homework before a big-game hunt can save a lot of time and effort once you've bagged your animal. And it will insure that the meat you bring home will be in prime condition for the table.

Familiarize yourself with state and local regulations. Some states prohibit quartering and skinning in the field; others require that you turn in certain parts for biological study. Be sure to check the regulations booklet available with your license. For more information, contact state or federal wildlife-management agencies.

If you are hunting for a trophy, consult in advance with a reliable taxidermist. He can give you advice on the best ways to handle the head and antlers in the field. There are also several good do-it-yourself kits for antler mounting and hide tanning.

The hides of deer, moose, and elk make excellent leather. Many tanneries will buy raw hides directly from hunters. If you plan on selling the hide, find out how the buyer wants it prepared. Some tanneries will exchange a raw hide for a pair of finished leather gloves. Or, you may want to have the hide tanned and returned to you.

Unless you have a reliable cold-storage area for holding your animal prior to butchering, make arrangements with a locker plant before you hunt. Ask about the locker's business hours; you don't want to return from hunting on a warm Saturday only to discover the plant is closed for the weekend.

HANG field-dressed big game in a tree to speed its cooling. Hanging also helps protect it from scavenging animals if you must leave to get help carrying it out. Use a block and tackle (inset) for easier lifting.

EQUIPMENT for field dressing includes: (1) folding lock-back knife and a spare, (2) small whetstone or sharpening stick, (3) several foot-long pieces of kitchen string, (4) two clean sponges, (5) zip-lock plastic bags, (6) rubber gloves, (7) block and tackle, and (8) 20 feet of ¼-inch nylon rope. If hunting moose or elk, also bring (9) cloth bags for carrying out the quarters if skinned, and (10) a belt axe or folding game saw for quartering. Hooks (11) can be slipped over the edges of the split ribcage, then tied to trees to hold the body open while gutting. Stow everything but the belt axe in your pack, along with a first-aid kit and other hunting gear.

In the Field

Before you shoot, consider the location and body position of the animal. Remember that you'll have to get it out of the area after it's down. If you spot an animal across a canyon, consider possible drag routes before shooting. A moose standing in a bog may be a tempting target, but you would probably need several people to move it to dry land for field dressing and quartering.

Shot placement affects both the quality and quantity of the meat you bring home. A study at Texas A&M University showed that game killed instantly with a clean shot produces meat more tender and flavorful than game only wounded with the first shot. Game animals, like humans, produce adrenalin and other chemicals when frightened or stressed. These chemicals make the meat tough and gamey. A poorly placed shot may also damage choice cuts, or rupture the stomach or intestines, tainting the meat.

If possible, shoot an animal that's standing still rather than running. A shot in the heart or neck will drop it instantly, and you'll lose little meat.

Approach a downed animal with caution, keeping your gun loaded and staying away from the hooves and antlers. Nudge the animal with your foot, or gently touch your gun barrel to its eye. If there's any reaction, shoot it in the head or heart. When certain the animal is dead, unload your gun and place it safely out of the way.

Field-dress the animal immediately to drain off the blood and dissipate the body heat. Wear rubber gloves to protect you from any parasites or blood-borne diseases the animal may be carrying, and to make cleanup easier.

The step-by-step instructions on the following pages will guide you through a field-dressing procedure that produces a clean carcass. Splitting the pelvis is optional with this method. In warm weather, you may wish to split the pelvis, because the hams cool faster when separated. However, an animal with a split pelvis is more difficult to drag. The separated hind legs flop around, and the cavity may get dirty.

If you elect to split the pelvis, cut between the hams as described. Then, locate the natural seam between the two halves of the pelvic bone, and cut through it with your knife. On a large or old animal, you may need to use a game saw or hatchet. Some hunters stand their knife upright with its tip on the seam, then strike the knife with their palm to split the pelvis. Do not attempt this unless you have a sturdy knife; you could damage the blade.

Be sure to follow state regulations requiring evidence of the sex left on the carcass. Antlers are usually adequate to identify a buck; in some states, antlers must be a certain length for the animal to be legal.

Where the law allows, attach the registration tag after field dressing, rather than before. The tag may get ripped off during the dressing procedure.

HUNTING KNIVES include general-purpose types, such as (1) folding drop-point and (2) folding clip-point. The tip of a clip-point is more acute and curves up higher than that of a drop-point; see inset photo, opposite page.

Special-purpose types include (3) folding bird knife, with a hook for field-dressing birds, as shown on page 38; (4) folding combination knife, with a blunt-tip blade for slitting abdomens without puncturing intestines, a clip-point

Selecting & Sharpening Hunting Knives

A good hunting knife is one of the best investments a hunter can make. Properly selected, used, and cared for, it may well outlive him. A cheap knife, on the other hand, may not last a single hunting season.

When selecting a hunting knife, look closely at the materials, blade length and shape, and workmanship.

The blade steel should be stainless, hard but not brittle. A blade with a *Rockwell hardness rating* of 57 to 60 is hard enough to hold an edge, but soft enough for easy resharpening at home when it does become dull.

The handle should be made of hardwood, plastic-impregnated wood, or a tough synthetic. These materials last longer than brittle plastic, or than wood you can easily dent with your fingernail.

Select a knife that feels comfortable in your hand. Remember that your hands may be wet when you're using it, and look for a handle shape that's easy to hold firmly. A blade between 3½ and 4½ inches long is adequate for either big or small game.

How to Sharpen a Knife

SELECT a medium whetstone at least as long as the blade. (If the blade is extremely dull, use a coarse stone first, then the medium stone.) Place the stone on a folded towel for stability, and apply a little honing oil.

HOLD the base of the blade against the whetstone at the angle at which the blade was originally sharpened (usually between 12 and 17 degrees). Using moderate pressure, push the knife away from you in a smooth arc from base to tip, as if shaving thin pieces off the face of the stone. Keep the edge of the blade at the same angle, in constant contact with the whetstone. Repeat this pushing motion two more times.

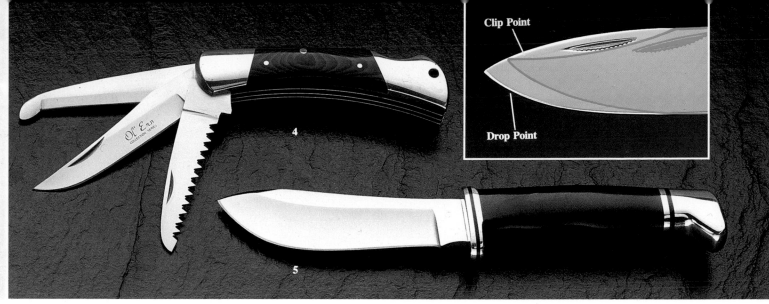

blade, and a saw for cutting through the breastbones and pelvic bones of big game; and (5) big-game skinner, whose blade has a blunt tip to avoid punching holes in the hide. The sides of the skinner blade are *concave,* curving down to a thin edge that's ideal for skinning but prone to chipping when used to cut against wood or bone. The other blades shown have sides that slant down straight, with thicker, sturdier edges.

Clip-point and *drop-point* knives (see inset photo above) are good all-purpose types. The acutely pointed tip of a clip-point is good for delicate cutting, and penetrates the abdominal skin easily in field dressing. The tip of a drop-point is less apt to puncture the intestines when slitting the abdominal skin, or to punch a hole in the hide should you use it for skinning.

For convenience and safety in the field, many hunters prefer folding knives. They are shorter and easier to carry than a straight knife, and the folded blade is safely out of the way in the event of a fall. Choose folding knives carefully, checking for quality construction. When fully opened, the blade should lock in position with no trace of wiggle or sloppiness, and the back of the blade should line up exactly with the back edge of the handle.

Use your knife only for its intended purpose. If you use it to hack wood or pry the lid off a jar, you could destroy the edge. Be sure your knife is clean and dry before you store it at the end of the season. Over time, even modern stainless steel can be corroded by salts or acids.

A sharp blade is safer than a dull one. It gives you more control, and you need less pressure to get the job done. Dress the edge often with a sharpening steel (page 21). A steel does not remove metal from the blade, but simply realigns the edge. When the blade becomes so dull that the steel won't dress it, sharpen it with a whetstone.

DRAW the knife toward you in an arc three times, maintaining the same angle. Continue sharpening alternate sides, adding oil if necessary, until the blade hangs up when drawn very gently over a fingernail.

REPEAT the previous steps on a fine whetstone. If the stone clogs, wipe and re-oil it. The knife is sharp when it slices effortlessly through a piece of paper. Clean the whetstone with soapy water for storage.

HANDY sharpening devices include (1) pre-angled sharpening kits; (2) ceramic sticks, which have a light sharpening action; and (3) diamond-impregnated sticks, which remove as much metal as a medium stone.

1. LOCATE the base of the breastbone by pressing on the center of the ribcage until you feel its end. Make a shallow cut that is long enough to insert the first two fingers of your left hand. Be careful not to puncture the intestines when cutting.

2. FORM a V with the first two fingers of your left hand. Hold the knife between your fingers with the cutting edge up, as shown. Cut through the abdominal wall to the pelvic area. Your fingers prevent you from puncturing the intestines.

3. SEPARATE the external reproductive organs of a buck from the abdominal wall, but do not cut them off completely. Remove the udder of a doe if it was still nursing. The milk sours rapidly, and could give the meat an unpleasant flavor.

14. SPONGE cavity clean, and prop open with a stick. If the urinary tract or intestines have been severed, wash meat with snow or clean water. If you must leave the animal, drape it over brush or logs with the cavity down, or hang it from a tree to speed cooling.

Anatomy of a Male Whitetail Deer

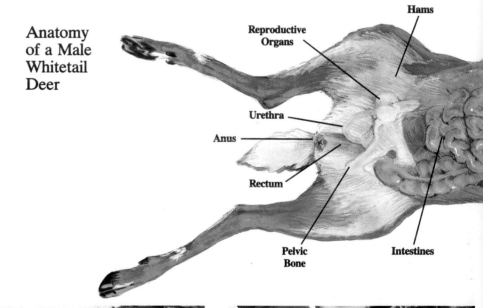

Hams

Reproductive Organs

Urethra

Anus

Rectum

Pelvic Bone

Intestines

13. GRASP the windpipe and esophagus firmly. Pull down and away from the animal's body. If the organs do not pull away freely, the diaphragm may still be partially attached. Scoop from both ends toward the middle to finish rolling out the entrails.

12. PULL tied-off rectum and urethra underneath the pelvic bone and into the body cavity, unless you have split the pelvic bone. (If you have, this is unnecessary.) Roll the animal on its side so the entrails begin to spill out the side of the body cavity.

11. CUT the tubes that attach the liver and remove it. Check liver for spots, cysts, or scarring, which could indicate parasites or disease. If you see any, discard the liver. If liver is clean, place into plastic bag with heart. Place on ice as soon as possible.

4. STRADDLE the animal, facing its head. Unless you plan to mount the head, cut the skin from the base of the breastbone to the jaw, with the cutting edge of the knife up. If you plan to mount the head, follow your taxidermist's instructions.

5. BRACE your elbows against your legs, with your left hand supporting your right. Cut through the center of the breastbone, using your knees to provide leverage. If the animal is old or very large, you may need to use a game saw or small axe.

6. SLICE between the hams to free a buck's urethra, or if you elect to split the pelvic bone on either a buck or doe. Make careful cuts around the urethra until it is freed to a point just above the anus. Be careful not to sever the urethra.

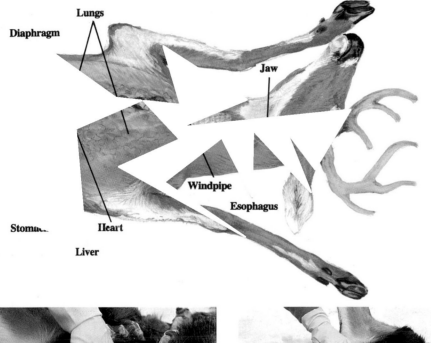

Lungs

Diaphragm

Jaw

Windpipe

Esophagus

Stomach

Heart

Liver

7. CUT around the anus; on a doe, the cut should also include the reproductive opening (above the anus). Free the rectum and urethra by loosening the connective tissue with your knife. Tie off the rectum and urethra with kitchen string (inset).

10. REMOVE the heart by severing the connecting blood vessels. Hold the heart upside down for a few moments to drain excess blood. Place heart in a plastic bag. Some hunters find it easier to remove the entrails first, then take the heart and liver from the gutpile.

9. HOLD ribcage open on one side with left hand. Cut the diaphragm, from the rib opening down to the backbone. Stay as close to the ribcage as possible; do not puncture the stomach. Repeat on other side so the cuts meet over the backbone.

8. FREE the windpipe and esophagus by cutting the connective tissue. Sever windpipe and esophagus at the jaw. Grasp them firmly and pull down, continuing to cut where necessary, until freed to the point where the windpipe branches out into the lungs.

Transporting Big-Game Animals

After field dressing, move the animal to camp as soon as possible. Leave the hide on to protect the meat from dirt and flies. The hide will also prevent the surface from drying too much during aging (page 17). In hot weather, however, you may want to remove the hide in the field to help cool the carcass.

If you plan to skin the animal in the field, bring along a large cloth bag or sheet to keep the meat clean during transport. Never put the carcass or quarters in plastic bags unless the meat is thoroughly chilled. The plastic traps the body heat, and the meat may be ruined. Avoid plastic garbage bags; they may be treated with a toxic disinfectant.

You may have to quarter an elk or moose to transport it from the field (opposite page). Some hunters skin the animal before quartering, so the hide can be tanned in one piece. Others prefer to quarter the animal first. A quartered hide is still suitable for tanning; in fact, most tanneries split whole elk or moose hides in half to make them easier to handle.

Wear blaze-orange clothing and make lots of noise when you move an animal in the field. Hunters have been known to mistakenly shoot at animals being dragged or carried. For this reason, the traditional method of carrying a deer, by lashing it to a pole between two hunters, is not recommended. If you must carry an animal this way, drape it completely with blaze-orange cloth.

Once in camp, hang the animal up (pages 16-17). Hanging aids cooling and blood drainage, and the stretching helps tenderize the meat. Clean the clots and excess blood from the heart and liver, then place them in plastic bags on ice.

Ideally, the carcass should be cooled to 40°F within 24 hours. Cool it as rapidly as possible, but don't allow it to freeze. The meat loses moisture if frozen and thawed, and the carcass is difficult to skin when frozen even partially. If the days are warm and the nights cool, keep the carcass covered with a sleeping bag during the day. If the nights are warm as well, store the carcass at a locker plant.

The best way to transport the animal home is in a closed trailer or covered pickup. In cool, dry weather, you can carry an animal on top of your car, with the head forward. Do not carry an animal on the hood, because heat from the engine will spoil the meat. If your trip is long and hot, pack bags of dry ice around the carcass. Or, quarter the animal, wrap well in plastic, and pack it into coolers with ice. Be sure to check state laws regarding transport of big game.

DRAG a deer with each front leg tied to an antler to keep from snagging brush. If the deer is antlerless, tie a rope around the neck. Snow makes dragging easier. If the terrain is dusty, sew the carcass shut with a cord after punching a hole in each side of the rib cage. A bear may be dragged on a heavy tarp, to avoid damaging the fur.

PILE quarters onto a horse, all-terrain vehicle, or snowmobile. Skinned quarters should be wrapped in cloth bags. Quarters from smaller animals can be strapped to a pack frame and packed out one at a time. If the quarters have not been skinned and the terrain is smooth, they can be dragged out as shown on the opposite page.

How to Quarter an Elk or Moose (pictured: Elk)

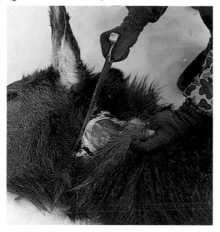

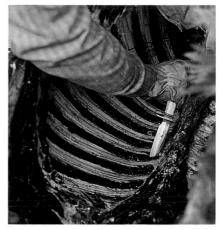

BEND a leg sharply, then cut the skin around the joint to remove the lower leg. Repeat on all legs.

SAW off the head after skinning the neck area. Sawing it before skinning would force hair into the meat.

CUT between the third and fourth ribs, from the backbone to the tips of the ribs. Cut from inside the body.

SEPARATE the front half of the animal from the rear half by sawing through the backbone.

SPLIT the hide along the backbone on both halves, then peel it back several inches on each side of the cut.

PROP one half against your legs, then begin sawing lengthwise through the backbone.

CONTINUE cutting while keeping the back off the ground. Gravity will help pull the quarters apart, making the cutting easier. Your saw will not bind, as it would if the half were lying on the ground.

QUARTERED elk looks like this. Depending on the animal's size, elk quarters weigh 60 to 125 pounds each; moose, up to 225 pounds. Where the law allows, some hunters bone the animal in the field to reduce weight.

DRAG out a hindquarter by punching a hole behind the last rib, then threading a rope through and tying as pictured. This way, you drag with the grain of the hair. To drag out a forequarter, tie a rope tightly around the neck.

Hanging, Aging, & Skinning Big Game

How should I hang my animal — from the head or by the hind legs? And what about aging — does it improve the meat or spoil it? If I'm going to age the animal, should I leave the hide on during aging or take it off? These questions cause a great deal of debate among hunters.

If you want the head for a trophy, the first question is answered for you: the animal must be hung by the hind legs. Many hunters hang all big game this way, and the U.S. Department of Agriculture recommends this method for butchering beef. Hanging by the hind legs allows the blood to drain from the choice hindquarters. If your animal must be hung outdoors, however, it's better to hang it from the head because of the direction of hair growth. Otherwise, the upturned hair would trap rain and snow.

Many laboratory and taste tests have demonstrated that aging will definitely tenderize the meat. The special tenderness and flavor of beef prime rib result from extended aging. Wild game can benefit in the same way. It's a matter of personal taste: some prefer the aged flavor and tenderness, others don't. Aging is unnecessary if all the meat will be ground into sausage or burger.

How to Hang an Animal by the Hind Legs (pictured: Deer)

MAKE a *gambrel* out of a 3-foot-long 2 × 2. Cut a shallow notch all around the wood an inch from each end, and another in the middle.

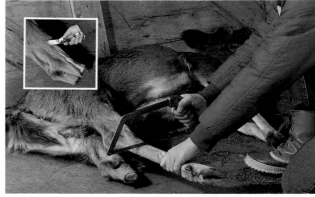

SAW off the bottom of each hind leg several inches below the knee. Cutting from inside the skin, slit the skin on each leg to a point about 4 inches above the knee (inset).

PEEL the skin over the leg to uncover the large tendon at the back of the leg. Then slit any tissue between the bone and the large tendon. The tendon is needed for hanging the animal, so be careful not to sever it.

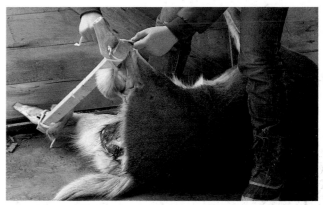

INSERT the gambrel in the slits. Tie each leg to the wood, wrapping the rope in the notch. Tie 6 feet of rope to the center notch, then loop it over a sturdy beam or through a pulley. Hoist the deer completely off the ground.

To prevent unwanted bacterial growth during the aging process, the carcass temperature must be stabilized between 35° and 40°F. If it fluctuates widely, condensation may form. Temperatures above 40° promote excess bacterial growth and cause the fat to turn rancid. If you age the animal outdoors or in a shed, be prepared to butcher it immediately or take it to a locker should the weather turn warm.

Leave the hide on during aging, if possible. It helps stabilize the temperature of the meat, and also reduces dehydration. In a study at the University of Wyoming, an elk carcass was cut in half down the backbone; one half was skinned, the other was not. After two weeks of aging, the skinned side lost over 20 percent more moisture. Animals aged without the hide will have a great deal of dried, dark meat to be trimmed, further reducing your yield.

During aging, enzyme activity breaks down the connective tissue that makes meat tough. Elk has more connective tissue than deer, antelope, or bear, and

can be aged longer. Antelope is probably the most tender of these animals; extended aging may give it a mushy texture. Many people prefer their antelope aged only about 3 days. Bear can age from 3 days to a week. Deer and cow elk reach their prime in a week to 10 days, and bull elk require up to 14 days. These times are for *ideal* conditions. Do not attempt to age an animal in warm conditions.

Some people prefer to quarter their meat, wrap the quarters in cloth, then age them in a refrigerator or old chest-style pop cooler. The effects are almost the same as hanging a whole carcass. The meat may be slightly less tender, because it doesn't get stretched as much.

If you prefer not to age the animal, delay butchering for at least 24 hours, until the carcass has cooled and the muscles have relaxed. The cuts will be ragged and unappealing if you start before cooling is complete, and the meat will be tough if butchered while the muscles are still contracted.

Skinning Big Game

Skinning is easiest while the animal is still warm. If you age the meat, however, it's best to leave the skin on until butchering.

Most hunters skin their animals by hand. The task isn't difficult, requiring only a knife and a saw. For easiest skinning, hang the animal from a pulley. Then you can raise or lower the carcass, so the area you're working on will always be at eye level. Or, hoist the animal on a rope running through a heavy-duty screw eye fastened to a solid ceiling beam.

Try to keep hair off the meat during skinning. Keep your knife sharp, touching it up as necessary with a steel or stone. Cut through the skin from the inside out, so your knife slips between the hairs. This way, you avoid cutting hairs in half or driving them into the meat, and your knife won't dull as quickly.

If you have several animals to skin, it may be worthwhile to set up a system for skinning with mechanical power. The photo sequence at the bottom of the opposite page shows how to skin a deer with a car. You can use the same method with a winch. But don't try to skin your animal mechanically if it's shot through the spine or neck; it could break apart.

After skinning, lay the hide out on a piece of plywood, skin side up. If you take a few moments to scrape off any bits of meat or fat, you will get a better piece of leather.

Most tanneries prefer to receive a hide salted and rolled. To protect it from rain and animals during the salting process, find a sheltered spot like a shed or garage. Sprinkle the skin side liberally with salt, and rub some into the edges, cuffs, and neck area. Tilt the plywood slightly so the hide will drain.

After a day, add more salt and fold the hide in half, skin side in. Roll the folded hide into a bundle and tie it with twine. Don't put the rolled hide in plastic, except for shipping, because it may rot. Keep it cold, and get it to the tannery as soon as possible.

If you have a deer hide, save the tail. It can be used for jig and fly tying, and hide buyers may pay several dollars for it.

If you're not going to butcher the animal yourself, deliver the carcass to the butcher with the hide still on, and let him skin it.

How to Skin an Animal Hanging by the Hind Legs (pictured: Antelope)

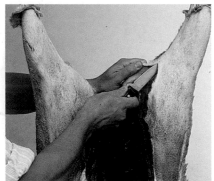

CUT the hide along the inner side of each hind leg. Note that the cut is made from the inside of the skin.

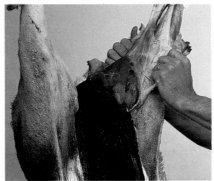

PEEL the hide away from the legs. Continue peeling until both legs are skinned and you reach the tail.

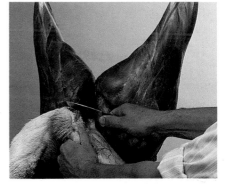

SEVER the tailbone close to the animal's rump. Leave the tailbone inside the skin.

CONTINUE peeling, using your fist to free the hide along the back. Use a knife only where necessary; take care not to cut a hole in the hide.

SAW off front legs just above the joint, after cutting along the inside of each leg and peeling the hide. Keep skinning until you reach the head.

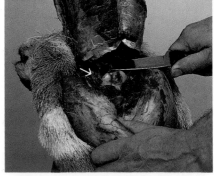

CUT off the head at the Atlas joint (arrow). First, make a deep cut around the neck at the base of the skull. Twist the head to pop the Atlas joint.

How to Skin an Animal Hanging from the Head *(pictured: Deer)*

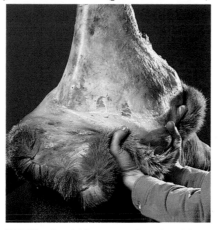

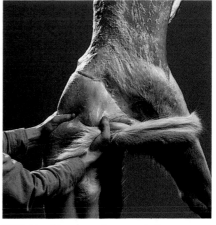

CUT the skin around the base of the head. Then peel the hide away from the neck with your fingers, using a knife only where necessary.

PEEL the hide over the shoulders. Saw off the front legs above the joint, as described on the opposite page. Pull the hide off the front legs.

KEEP skinning down to the rump. Sever the tailbone; cut off hind legs above knee. Cut hide along inside of each leg. Pull hide completely off.

How to Skin an Animal with Mechanical Power *(pictured: Deer)*

HANG the animal from the head on a sturdy tree. Remove the lower portion of each leg. Cut the skin around the neck, and peel back about 6 inches. Then, cut the skin along the inside of each leg, up to the body cavity.

PLACE a golf ball or small rounded rock under the peeled neck skin. Gather the skin around it, and tie off tightly with strong cord. Fasten the cord to a secure part of a vehicle, or to a winch.

BEGIN driving slowly away from the animal. If using a winch, crank steadily. The hide will begin peeling off. If the hide seems hard to pull, you may have to start it over the shoulders by hand.

CONTINUE driving until skinning is complete. Once the hide is past the shoulders, the rest comes off easily. More fat and meat will probably remain on the hide than if you had skinned it by hand.

Butchering Big Game

When you do your own butchering, you know that the meat has been handled with care, and you get the cuts you prefer. You will probably be willing to take more time trimming than a butcher would, so your finished cuts may have less gristle, fat, and silverskin on them.

In most cases, the animal is butchered while still hanging from the skinning process. Use caution when butchering a hanging animal. When you cut off each portion, you must "catch" it, and this can be tricky with a knife in one hand. A deer leg, for instance, may weigh 20 pounds or more, so you may need a partner to catch it. Be absolutely certain that your partner stays clear of your knife, and never allow him to cut at the same time. For safety, some hunters prefer to butcher on a large table.

The photo sequence on pages 22 and 23 shows how to cut up a deer that is hanging from the head. The procedure is somewhat different if the animal is hanging by the hind legs. You will not be able to cut off the hind legs because they are supporting the carcass. Instead, remove the front legs, backstrap, and ribs as described, then place the hindquarters on a table to finish cutting.

After cutting up the carcass, bone the meat. Boning is easier than bone-in butchering, and usually results in tastier meat. Bone marrow is fatty and can turn rancid, even in the freezer. By boning, you avoid cutting the bones, so there is no bone residue to affect the meat's flavor. In addition, boned meat takes less freezer space and is easier to wrap. There are no sharp edges to puncture the freezer wrap and expose the meat to freezer burn.

On pages 24 and 25, you'll learn an easy method for boning a big-game animal. To roughly estimate the amount of boned meat you will get, divide the field-dressed weight of your animal in half. You will get a smaller yield if the shot damaged much meat, or if you aged the animal.

Work on a large hardwood or plexiglass cutting board. To keep bacterial growth to a minimum, wash the board with a solution of 3 tablespoons of household bleach to 1 gallon of water, and wash it occasionally during the boning process. Keep two large bowls handy for the trimmings. As you bone, place large chunks to be used for stew in one bowl; small scraps for sausage or burger in the other.

How you make the final boning cuts depends on the animal's size. On a moose, for instance, the rump portion is large enough to yield several roasts. But on an antelope, the same cut is too small for a roast, and is better for steaks, kabobs, or stroganoff.

Keep the meat cool throughout the butchering and boning process. Work on the carcass in a cool shed or garage. To reduce bacterial growth, bone and freeze each portion as you remove it, or refrigerate it until you can bone it. You can butcher faster by working in pairs; while one person cuts up the carcass, the other works on boning.

Save the bones if you want to make soup or stock (pages 69 and 144). The backbone makes particularly good stock. Saw the larger bones into pieces to fit your stockpot.

EQUIPMENT for butchering big game includes (1) hunting or boning knife, (2) sharpening steel or whetstone, (3) heavy-duty plastic wrap, (4) freezer paper, (5) freezer tape, (6) waterproof marking pen, (7) game or meat saw, (8) kitchen scale.

DRESS your knife frequently with a sharpening steel. Hold the base of the blade against the steel at the angle at which it was originally sharpened. Draw the knife toward you in an arc from base to tip. Repeat on other side. Alternate sides until the blade is sharp.

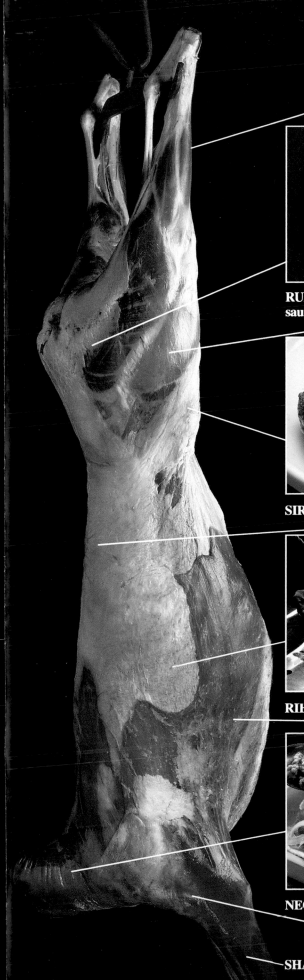

SHANK: Soups, stock, burger, sausage, jerky

RUMP: Kabobs, steaks, roasts, sautées, grilling

BOTTOM and TOP ROUNDS: Roasts, steaks, sautées, kabobs

SIRLOIN TIP: Steaks, roasts

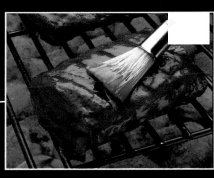

BACKSTRAP: Grilling, butterflied steaks, sautées

RIBS: Ribs, burger, sausage

BRISKET and TRIMMINGS: Burger, sausage, jerky, corning

SHOULDER: Jerky, pot roasts, stews, burger, sausage

NECK: Sausage, burger, pot roasts

SHANK

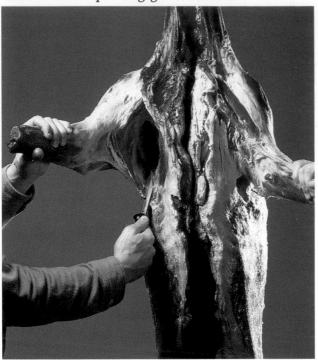

1. PUSH the front leg away from the body, then begin cutting between the leg and the ribcage. Continue until you reach the shoulder. It helps to have someone steady the carcass, but make sure he or she is safely away from your knife.

2. REMOVE the front leg by cutting between the shoulder blade and the back. Repeat with the other leg. Remove the layer of brisket meat over the ribs (inset). Moose or elk brisket is thick enough to be rolled for corning (page 85). Grind thin brisket for burger.

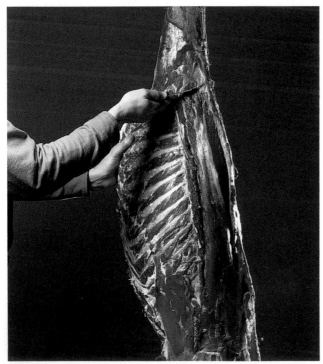

3. CUT the meat at the base of the neck to begin removing a *backstrap*. There are two backstraps, one on each side of the spine. Backstraps can be butterflied for steaks (page 53), cut into roasts, or sliced thinly for sautéeing. The lower part, or *loin,* is most tender.

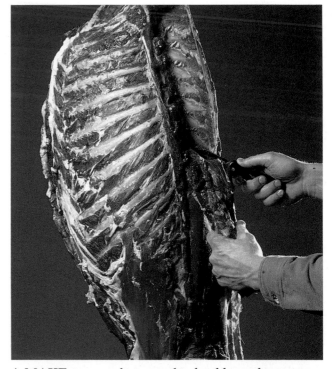

4. MAKE two cuts between the shoulder and rump: one along the spine, the other along the rib tops. Keep your knife close to the bones, removing as much meat as possible. Cut off this first backstrap at the rump, then remove the backstrap on the other side of the spine.

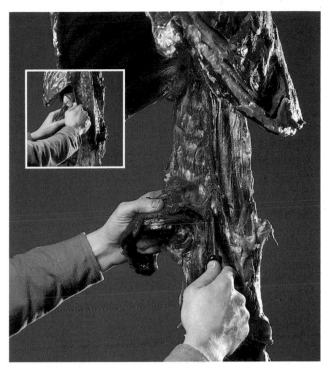

5. BEGIN cutting one hind leg away, exposing the ball-and-socket joint (arrow). Push the leg back to pop the joint apart, then cut through the joint. Work your knife around the tailbone and pelvis until the leg is removed. Repeat with the other leg.

6. CUT the *tenderloins* from inside the body cavity after trimming the flank meat below the last rib (inset). The flank meat can be ground, or cut into thin strips for jerky. Many hunters remove the tenderloins before aging the animal, to keep them from darkening and dehydrating.

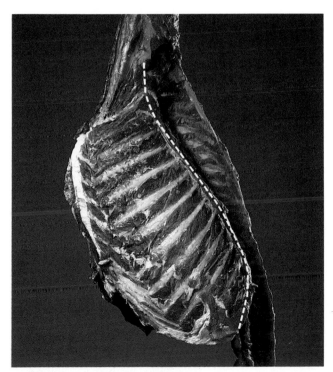

7. REMOVE the ribs if desired by sawing along the backbone (dotted lines). Cut around the base of the neck, then twist the backbone off. Separate the neck and head (page 18). Bone the neck to grind for burger, or keep it whole for pot roasting.

8. TRIM the ribs by cutting away the ridge of meat and gristle along the bottom. If the ribs are long, saw them in half. Cut ribs into racks of three or four. If you don't want to save the ribs, you can bone the meat between them and grind it for burger or sausage.

How to Bone a Hind Leg (pictured: Antelope)

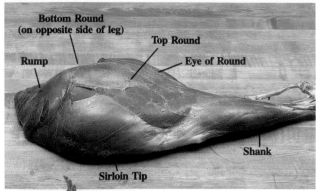

A HIND LEG consists of the sirloin tip, the top and bottom rounds, the eye of round, a portion of the rump, and the shank. The sirloin, rounds, and rump are tender cuts for roasting or grilling; the shank is tough, and best for ground meat or soups.

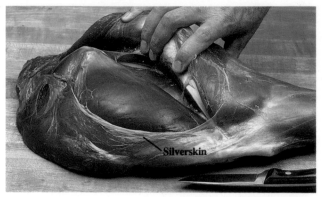

SEPARATE the *top round* from the rest of the leg after cutting through the thin layer of silverskin that covers the leg. Work your fingers into the natural seam, then begin pulling the top round away from the leg. Use your knife only where necessary to free the meat.

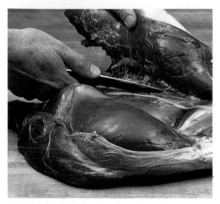

CUT along the back of the leg to remove the top round completely. The top round is excellent when butterflied, rolled and tied for roasting (see opposite page). Or, cut it into two smaller flat roasts, cube for kabobs, or slice for sautées.

REMOVE the *rump* portion. Cut the rump off at the top of the hipbone after removing the silverskin and pulling the muscle groups apart with your fingers. A large rump is excellent for roasting; a small one can be cut for steaks, kabobs, or sautées.

CUT *bottom round* away from *sirloin tip* after turning leg over and separating these two muscle groups with your fingers. Next, carve sirloin tip away from bone. Sirloin tip makes a choice roast or steaks; bottom round is good for roasting, steaks, or kabobs.

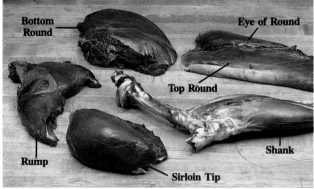

A BONED LEG will look like this. Cut the *shank* and upper leg bone apart at the knee joint if you plan on using the shank for soup. Or, cut the meat off the shank close to the bone; trim away the tendons and silverskin, and grind the meat for burger or sausage. Use the leftover bones for stock (page 144). On a larger animal, you may wish to separate the *eye of round* from the top round.

MAKE large-diameter steaks from a whole hind leg by cutting across all the muscle groups rather than boning as described above. First, remove the rump portion as described, then cut the leg into inch-thick steaks. As each steak is cut, work around the bone with a fillet knife, then slide the steak over the end of the bone. Continue steaking until you reach the shank.

How to Bone a Front Leg (pictured: Deer)

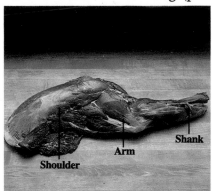

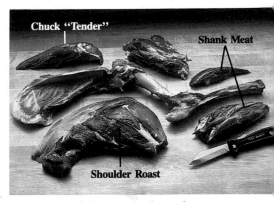

A FRONT LEG consists of the shoulder, arm, and shank. The meat from the front leg is less tender than that from the hind leg, and is used for pot roasting, stews, jerky, or grinding.

CUT along bony ridge in the middle of the shoulder blade. One side yields the small boneless chuck "tender." Bone the other side along the dotted line to make a shoulder roast.

TRIM remaining meat from bones. Use the chuck "tender" for jerky or stews. Pot roast the shoulder roast, cut into stew chunks, or use for jerky. Grind the shank meat for burger.

How to Make a Rolled Roast (pictured: Deer Bottom Round)

BUTTERFLY meat that is thicker than one inch by cutting into two thinner pieces; leave the meat connected at one edge. Open the butterflied meat up so it lies flat. Roll the meat tightly with the grain, tucking in any irregular edges.

TIE the rolled meat about an inch from the end that is farthest from you; use a 60" length of kitchen string. Leave several inches at the short end of the string; you will need to tie the two ends of the string together after making loops around the meat.

MAKE a loop in the string, then twist the loop once to make a small "braid" (arrow). Slip the braided loop over the end of the meat closest to you, then slide the loop so it is about one inch from the string tied around the far end.

SNUG up this first loop by pulling on the long end of the string, adjusting its length so the braid lines up with the original knot. The roast will look more attractive when it is served if all the braids are lined up along the top of the roast.

CONTINUE making loops about an inch apart, snugging them up as you go. Tie on additional string if necessary. When you have made a loop about an inch from the close end (dotted line), slip the string underneath the roast so it comes out on the far side.

TIE the two ends of the string together with a double overhand knot. Trim both ends of the string close to the knot. When you are ready to carve a cooked rolled roast, simply snip the loops along the top of the roast and pull off the string.

Antelope Round Steak
9/27

Deer tenderloins
9/27

Freezing Wild Game

Many hunters spend hours dressing and portioning their game, then hurriedly wrap it in a plastic bag and toss it in the freezer. When they defrost it, they're surprised to find their efforts were wasted, because the meat is dried out, or *freezer burned.*

To prevent freezer burn, double-wrap the meat or freeze it in water. This step is especially important if you own a modern frost-free freezer. In a freezer of this type, a fan unit pulls the moisture out of the air to prevent frost build-up. Unfortunately, it also pulls the moisture out of poorly wrapped meat.

Remove all fat from big game and raccoons before wrapping them for the freezer. The fat of these animals may turn rancid even while frozen, affecting the taste of the meat.

Backstraps, sirloin tips, and other choice boneless cuts of big game should not be steaked before freezing. Moisture escapes from each cut surface, so smaller pieces lose more moisture than bigger ones. Freeze the whole cut, or divide it into two or three pieces large enough for a family meal. This way, you can use a piece as a roast, or steak it after thawing.

The same principle applies to freezing stew, burger, or sausage meat. Freeze larger chunks, then cut them to size or grind them just before cooking. Game ground with fat for burger meat does not keep as long as plain ground meat, because the fat can turn rancid.

Mark all packages clearly with waterproof, permanent ink. Note the species of animal, the type of cut if applicable, the weight or number of servings, and the date. An old, potentially tough animal should be indicated as such. Some hunters mark with a different color of ink each season, so they can tell at a glance which packages are oldest.

To promote rapid freezing, arrange the wrapped packages in a single layer in the freezer, then turn the freezer to the coldest setting. Stack the packages only after they're frozen.

Thaw frozen game by placing the wrapped package on a plate in the refrigerator at least a full day before you want to cook the meat. The cool temperature minimizes bacterial growth, and the slow thaw helps tenderize the meat.

Freezer Storage Chart

TYPE OF MEAT	WRAPPING METHOD*	MAXIMUM STORAGE TIME
Big Game Roasts	Standard butcher wrap	10 months
Big Game Steaks	Standard butcher wrap	8 months
Big Game Ribs	Foil wrap	5 months
Big Game Organs	Standard butcher wrap Water pack	4 months 6 months
Big Game Chunks	Freezer bag and paper	6 months
Big Game Burger	Freezer bag and paper	4 months
Cut-up Small Game	Standard butcher wrap Water pack	8 months 1 year
Small Game Organs	Water pack	10 months
Whole Large Birds	Foil wrap	5 months
Whole Small Birds	Standard butcher wrap Water pack	6 months 1 year
Cut-up Upland Birds	Standard butcher wrap Water pack	8 months 1 year
Cut-up Waterfowl	Standard butcher wrap Water pack	8 months 1 year
Bird Giblets	Water pack	4 months
Game Stock	Freezer containers	4 months

*Photo instructions given for all wrapping techniques on pages 46-49.

The Standard Butcher Wrap

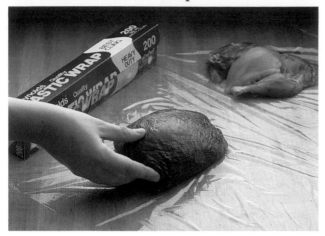

PLACE the meat on the center of a large piece of plastic wrap. If wrapping a cut-up bird or small-game animal, arrange the pieces to form a compact bundle, with as little space between them as possible.

BRING one end of the wrap over the meat, then fold both sides over it. Gently squeeze out as much air as possible. Bring the other end over, or roll the bundle to it, continuing to squeeze out air.

LAY the plastic-wrapped bundle on a corner of a large piece of heavy-duty freezer paper (shiny side up).

ROLL the bundle once, so both the top and bottom are covered with a single layer of freezer paper.

FOLD one side of the freezer paper over the bundle. Tuck in any loose edges of the paper.

ROLL the bundle again. Fold the other side of the freezer paper over the bundle, tucking the corner neatly.

FASTEN the end with freezer tape when wrapping is complete. Tape the seam also, if desired.

LABEL with a waterproof pen. Note the species, cut, quantity, date, and maturity of animal if noted.

The Foil Wrap

USE foil instead of plastic wrap for ribs or other odd-shaped cuts. Place the meat on a large piece of heavy-duty aluminum foil.

PRESS the foil around the meat to eliminate air spaces. Be careful not to puncture the foil with the bones. Use two pieces of foil if necessary.

BUTCHER-WRAP with freezer paper, eliminating as much air as possible. Seal all seams with freezer tape, and label the package.

How to Wrap a Whole Large Game Bird

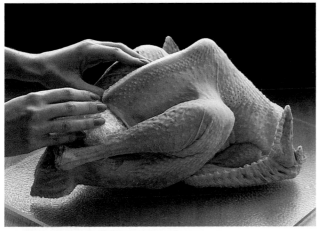

STUFF wadded plastic wrap into the body cavity. This reduces the chance of freezer burn.

TIE the drumsticks together with kitchen string. They'll stick out less, and wrapping will be easier.

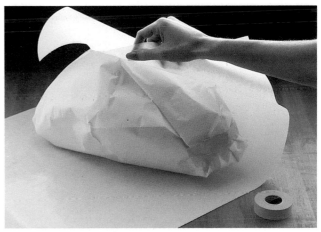

WRAP the bird with heavy-duty aluminum foil. You may need several pieces to cover the entire bird. Press the foil snugly around the body.

COMPLETE the wrapping with a double layer of heavy-duty freezer paper. Seal all the seams with freezer tape, and label the package.

SAVE waxed dairy cartons. Open up the tops, and wash the cartons well. Or, use plastic freezer containers. Square-bottomed containers make the best use of your freezer space.

PLACE game in cartons or plastic containers. Use pint- or quart-sized cartons for small whole birds, half-gallon cartons for large ones. Tiny birds like woodcock or doves can be frozen four to six per carton. Layer giblets in a small carton. Arrange cut-up birds or small game in a plastic container. Cover the game with water, jiggle it to eliminate air bubbles, and freeze.

CHECK after the water is frozen to be sure the game is completely covered with a layer of ice. If not, add cold water and refreeze.

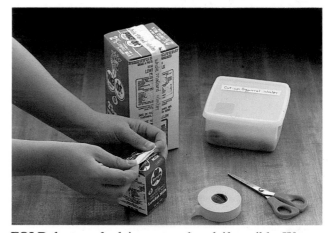

FOLD the top of a dairy carton closed, if possible. Wrap a band of freezer tape around the carton so it sticks to itself; label the tape. Label the lid of a plastic container.

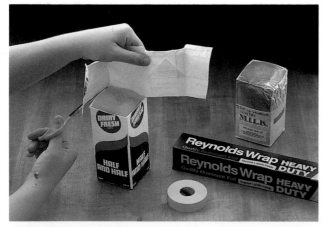

CUT off the top if the carton can't be closed, or if it isn't filled to the fold with ice. Trim at the ice level. Cover the top with heavy-duty aluminum foil. Wrap freezer tape around the edge of the foil, and label it.

ADD more giblets to the frozen ones as you shoot more birds. Place fresh giblets on top of the frozen ones. Add cold water; refreeze. Keep track of the number of giblets on a piece of tape, until you have enough for a meal.

How to Water-pack Cut-up Game in a Plastic Bag

PLACE a zip-lock plastic freezer bag in a cake pan, then arrange the pieces in the bag. The bag should lie on its side in the pan.

ADD water to completely cover the pieces of game. Squeeze out all the air, and seal the top of the bag. Set the pan in the freezer.

BUTCHER-WRAP the frozen bag with freezer paper. This keeps it from ripping or puncturing, which could open the meat to freezer burn.

Tips for Freezing Game

TRIPLE-WRAP cut steaks or chops for additional protection from freezer burn. Use two layers of plastic wrap, then finish with a layer of freezer paper.

TUCK the legs of a partridge, quail, or other small bird into the body cavity before wrapping. The package will be more compact, with less air inside to dry the meat.

PUT stew chunks or ground meat in a zip-lock plastic freezer bag. To push out air, immerse the bag almost to its top in a sinkful of cold water. Seal the bag while it's still in the water. Wrap it in freezer paper.

FREEZE 1-cup batches of cooked game stock in small dairy cartons or plastic freezer containers. When a recipe calls for stock, take a carton from the freezer, hold it under warm water, then slide the frozen stock out.

← Big Game Baked Round Steak

This is a good "company" dish. Once the meat is in the oven, you are free to enjoy your guests. The finished steaks are very attractive, with a slightly barbecued appearance.

2 to 3 pounds boneless deer, antelope, elk, or moose round steak, 1 inch thick
½ cup all-purpose flour
2 teaspoons salt
¼ teaspoon pepper
1 to 2 tablespoons butter or margarine
2 to 3 tablespoons olive oil or vegetable oil
3 tablespoons finely chopped onion
    Brown sugar
    Catsup
    Dried basil leaves
1 tablespoon butter or margarine, cut up
¼ cup venison stock (page 144) or beef broth

6 to 8 servings

Heat oven to 350°. Trim meat; cut into serving-sized pieces. Pound to ½-inch thickness with meat mallet. On a sheet of waxed paper, mix flour, salt, and pepper. Dip steaks in flour mixture, turning to coat. In large skillet, melt 1 tablespoon butter in 2 tablespoons oil over medium-high heat. Add coated steaks; brown on both sides. Fry in two batches if necessary, adding additional butter and oil. Arrange browned steaks in 12×8-inch baking pan. Sprinkle with onion. Top each steak with 1 teaspoon packed brown sugar and 1 teaspoon catsup. Sprinkle lightly with basil. Dot with 1 tablespoon butter. Add stock to drippings in skillet. Cook over medium heat for about 1 minute, stirring to loosen any browned bits. Add to baking pan. Cover with aluminum foil. Bake for about 45 minutes. Remove foil. If meat appears dry, add a small amount of stock or water to pan. Bake until browned on top, about 15 minutes longer.

Fillet of Venison   LOW-FAT   VERY FAST

You may substitute a moose or elk tenderloin, or the loin portion of the backstrap from an antelope or deer, for the deer tenderloin in this recipe.

1 whole deer tenderloin, 1 to 3 pounds
1 to 2 tablespoons butter or margarine
1 tablespoon olive oil or vegetable oil
    Salt and freshly ground black pepper
    Madeira Game Sauce (page 147), optional

2 or 3 servings per pound

Remove all surface fat and silverskin from tenderloin. Slice across grain into 1-inch-thick fillets. In medium skillet, melt butter in oil over medium-low heat. Add fillets; cook to desired doneness over medium-high heat, turning once. Salt and pepper to taste. Serve with Madeira Game Sauce.

Grilled Loin with Brown Sugar Baste ◇ LOW-FAT ● FAST →

Thick big-game steaks are also excellent in this recipe.

2 to 4 pounds deer, antelope, elk, or moose loin
    portion or whole backstrap
3 tablespoons butter or margarine
3 tablespoons soy sauce
3 tablespoons packed brown sugar

2 or 3 servings per pound

Start charcoal briquets in grill. Remove all fat and silverskin from meat. Cut into lengths about 4 inches long, or about 6 to 8 ounces each. In small saucepan, melt butter over medium heat. Add soy sauce and brown sugar. Cook, stirring constantly, until brown sugar dissolves and sauce bubbles.

When charcoal briquets are covered with ash, spread them evenly in grill. Place grate above hot coals. Place meat on grate. Grill on one side until seared. Turn meat over; brush with brown sugar mixture. Continue grilling, brushing frequently with brown sugar mixture and turning occasionally to grill all sides, until desired doneness.

Big Game Swiss Steak ◇ LOW-FAT

Any big-game steak can be used with this method. The long, slow cooking tenderizes even tough cuts.

1½ pounds boneless deer round steak or other
    big-game steak, ½ to 1 inch thick
⅓ cup all-purpose flour
1 teaspoon salt
¼ teaspoon pepper
3 to 4 tablespoons bacon fat
1 can (16 ounces) stewed tomatoes
¾ cup water
1 teaspoon instant beef bouillon granules
½ teaspoon dried basil leaves
½ teaspoon dried marjoram leaves
1 medium onion, thinly sliced

4 to 6 servings

Trim meat; cut into serving-sized pieces. Pound to ¼- to ½-inch thickness with meat mallet. On a sheet of waxed paper, mix flour, salt, and pepper. Dip steaks in flour mixture, turning to coat. In large skillet, heat bacon fat over medium heat. Add coated steaks; brown lightly on both sides. Fry in two batches if necessary. In small mixing bowl, mix stewed tomatoes, water, bouillon granules, basil, and marjoram; pour over steaks. Top meat and tomatoes with sliced onion. Heat to boiling. Reduce heat; cover. Simmer over very low heat until meat is tender, 1½ to 2 hours. Skim fat if desired.

Bear Steak Flamade

This hearty dish is good after outdoor winter activities. Serve with mashed potatoes, homemade wheat bread, and colorful vegetables.

⅓ cup all-purpose flour
1 teaspoon salt
¼ teaspoon pepper
2 pounds bear round steak, 1 inch thick
½ cup butter or margarine, divided
2 tablespoons olive oil or vegetable oil
4 medium onions, thinly sliced
1½ cups beer
¼ teaspoon dried marjoram leaves
¼ teaspoon dried thyme leaves
1 bay leaf

6 to 8 servings

Heat oven to 325°. On a sheet of waxed paper, mix flour, salt, and pepper. Dip steak in flour mixture, turning to coat. In large skillet, melt ¼ cup butter in oil over medium-low heat. Add steak; brown on both sides over medium-high heat. Transfer meat and drippings to 3-quart casserole; set aside.

In large skillet, melt remaining ¼ cup butter over medium-low heat. Add onions, stirring to coat with butter. Cover. Cook until tender but not brown, about 10 minutes. Pour onions over steak in casserole. Add remaining ingredients. Cover. Bake until meat is tender, 2 to 2½ hours. Discard bay leaf before serving.

Old-Fashioned Venison Stew ◇ LOW-FAT ↓

1½ cups water
½ cup beer
2 envelopes (⅞ ounce each) onion gravy mix
1 tablespoon packed brown sugar
¼ teaspoon ground thyme
2 to 3 pounds deer, antelope, elk, or moose stew meat
3 tablespoons vegetable oil
1 bay leaf
6 carrots, cut into 1-inch pieces
6 medium parsnips, cut into 1-inch cubes
1 cup frozen peas

6 to 8 servings

In small mixing bowl, blend water, beer, gravy mix, brown sugar, and thyme. Set aside. Remove all fat and silverskin from meat. Cut into 1-inch pieces. In Dutch oven, brown meat in oil over medium-high heat. Add beer mixture and bay leaf to Dutch oven. Reduce heat; cover. Simmer until meat is almost tender, 1 to 1½ hours, stirring occasionally. Add carrots and parsnips; re-cover. Cook 20 minutes longer. Add peas; re-cover. Cook 5 to 10 minutes longer. Discard bay leaf before serving.

Zesty Venison Stew ◇ LOW-FAT

1 to 2 pounds deer, antelope, elk, or moose stew meat
1 medium onion, chopped
2 tablespoons vegetable oil
2 tablespoons catsup
2 tablespoons currant jelly
2 tablespoons Worcestershire sauce
1 teaspoon salt
¼ cup all-purpose flour
1½ cups venison stock (page 144) or beef broth
1 cup red wine
2 medium potatoes
1 cup sliced carrot
2 cups fresh cauliflowerets

3 to 6 servings

Remove all fat and silverskin from meat. Cut into 1-inch pieces. Set aside. In Dutch oven, cook and stir onion in oil over medium heat until tender. Add catsup, jelly, Worcestershire sauce, and salt. Stir to melt jelly. Blend in flour. Add meat, stock, and wine; stir well. Cover and simmer until meat is almost tender, 1 to 1½ hours. Peel potatoes and cut into 1-inch chunks. Add potatoes and carrot to stew. Cook 20 minutes longer. Add cauliflowerets. Cook until vegetables are tender, about 20 minutes longer.

Spicy Elk Kabobs  ◆ LOW-FAT →

Kabobs are also excellent cooked on a charcoal grill.

MARINADE:

¼ cup finely chopped onion
¼ cup white wine
2 tablespoons vegetable oil
2 tablespoons soy sauce
1 tablespoon packed brown sugar
2 teaspoons ground coriander
1 teaspoon chili powder
½ teaspoon salt
½ teaspoon lemon pepper seasoning
⅛ teaspoon crushed red pepper flakes

1 pound elk steak, cut into 1-inch cubes
2 cups water
1 medium zucchini (6 to 8 ounces), cut into
   ¾-inch slices
1 sweet red pepper, cut into 16 pieces

4 servings

In medium saucepan, combine all marinade ingredients. Heat to boiling, stirring occasionally. Cool to room temperature. Add elk cubes. Toss to coat with marinade. Cover; marinate at room temperature for 30 minutes.

While elk is marinating, heat water to boiling in medium saucepan. Add zucchini. Return to boiling. Boil 2 minutes. Drain and rinse under cold water.

With slotted spoon, lift elk cubes from marinade. Set marinade aside. Divide elk, zucchini, and pepper into four groups. For each kabob, alternate elk with zucchini and pepper on 12-inch kabob skewer. Arrange kabobs on broiler pan. Set oven to broil and/or 550°. Broil kabobs 2 to 3 inches from heat until meat is desired doneness, 6 to 12 minutes, turning kabobs and brushing with marinade once.

Variation: Substitute deer, antelope, or moose for the elk.

Grilled Bacon-Wrapped Big Game ● VERY FAST

Deer, antelope, elk, moose, or bear is excellent prepared in this simple fashion. Serve as a main course, or as an appetizer to a wild-game dinner.

1 to 1¼ pounds big-game round or rump pieces,
   ¾ to 1 inch thick
4 to 8 slices bacon

2 to 4 servings

Start charcoal briquets in grill. Cut meat into 2-inch-wide strips. Wrap one or two slices bacon around each strip. Secure bacon with toothpicks. When charcoal briquets are covered with ash, spread them in grill. Place grate above hot coals. Grill meat strips to desired doneness, 4 to 7 minutes per side.

Roasting Big Game

There are two basic ways to roast big game: with dry heat and moist heat. Dry-heat roasting includes high- and low-temperature methods. The most common method of moist-heat roasting is braising, which includes pot roasting.

Only prime roasts are candidates for dry-heat, high-temperature cooking. These include the top round, sirloin tip, backstrap, and rump roasts. The tenderloin of a moose, elk, or large deer may also be used. These prime cuts are naturally tender, and do not need long, slow cooking for tenderizing.

For high-temperature cooking, select a roast between 2 and 5 inches thick, or a thinner piece you can roll and tie (page 25). First, brown the meat in hot fat, then roast it in a hot (400° to 450°) oven. With these high temperatures, roasts should be cooked only rare to medium. If cooked well-done, they dry out and shrink.

Low-temperature roasting is another option for these same prime cuts. And it's necessary for such medium-tender cuts as the bottom round and eye of round, which need longer cooking to ensure tenderness. Cover the meat with bacon or a sheet of beef or pork fat (available from your butcher), or baste it frequently. Cook it in a slow (300° to 325°) oven. With low heat, roasts may be cooked rare, medium, or well-done.

When roasting with dry heat, use a meat thermometer to check for doneness. The chart below gives temperatures for various stages of doneness. Remove the meat from the oven when it reads 5° below the ideal temperature; it will continue to heat on the platter. It will slice better if you wait 10 to 15 minutes before carving.

Moist heat tenderizes shoulder roasts and other tough cuts, and also works well with the bottom round and eye of round. Brown the roast in hot fat, then add liquid and flavoring and cover the pan tightly. Cook the meat until tender, on the stove top or in a moderate (325° to 350°) oven. When pot-roasting, add vegetables during the last hour or so of cooking. Braised meat is always served well-done.

Internal Temperature of Meat at Various Degrees of Doneness

DEGREE OF DONENESS	INTERNAL TEMPERATURE
Rare	130° to 135°
Medium-rare	135° to 140°
Medium	140° to 145°
Medium-well	150° to 155°
Well-done	155° to 160°

Roast Boneless Sirloin Tip ◆ LOW-FAT

You may substitute a backstrap, rolled top round, or rump roast for the sirloin tip in this high-temperature method. Sirloin tip roasts from elk or moose may be too large to roast with this method.

1 boneless deer or antelope sirloin tip roast or other suitable roast, 2 to 5 inches thick
1 to 2 tablespoons olive oil or vegetable oil

2 to 4 servings per pound

Heat oven to 450°. In medium skillet or Dutch oven, sear roast well on all sides in oil over medium-high heat. Place on rack in roasting pan. Roast to desired doneness (see chart at bottom left), 18 to 28 minutes per pound; remove roast when temperature is 5° less than desired. Allow meat to rest for 10 to 15 minutes before carving.

Roast Big Game Tenderloin ◆LOW-FAT

In this combination of high- and low-temperature roasting, a whole tenderloin is seared in the oven, then roasted at a reduced temperature. You may substitute the loin from an antelope or deer.

1   whole elk, moose, or large deer tenderloin, 1½
    to 3½ pounds
    Peanut or vegetable oil
    Salt and freshly ground black pepper
1   recipe Madeira Game Sauce (page 147),
    optional

2 to 4 servings per pound

Heat oven to 450°. Place tenderloin in roasting pan; tuck small end under. Brush tenderloin with oil. Roast at 450° for 10 minutes. Reduce heat to 350°. Roast to desired doneness (see chart on opposite page), 20 to 25 minutes per pound; remove roast when temperature is 5° less than desired. Allow meat to rest for 10 minutes before carving. Sprinkle with salt and pepper. Serve with Madeira Game Sauce.

Peppered Antelope Roast ↑

This recipe uses the low-temperature roasting method. Substitute a deer or small elk sirloin tip; deer, elk, or moose backstrap or rump roast; or antelope or deer bottom round.

2   medium cloves garlic
1   boneless rolled antelope or deer top round
    roast or other suitable roast, 3 to 5 pounds
    Vegetable oil
    Cracked black pepper
8 to 10 slices bacon

2 to 4 servings per pound

Heat oven to 325°. Cut each garlic clove into 4 or 5 slivers. Make 8 or 10 shallow slits in roast. Insert a garlic sliver into each slit. Place roast on rack in roasting pan; brush with oil. Sprinkle pepper liberally over roast. Cover roast with bacon slices. Roast to desired doneness (see chart on opposite page), 22 to 32 minutes per pound; remove roast when temperature is 5° less than desired. Allow meat to rest for 10 to 15 minutes before carving. Serve with pan juices.

Venison Roast Burgundy ◆ LOW-FAT ↓

2 tablespoons all-purpose flour
1 cup burgundy
½ teaspoon dried rosemary leaves
½ teaspoon dried marjoram leaves
½ teaspoon salt
¼ teaspoon pepper
3 to 4-pound deer, elk, or moose roast
4 carrots, cut into 2-inch pieces
2 medium onions, quartered
2 bay leaves
1 tablespoon cornstarch
¼ cup cold water
½ teaspoon brown bouquet sauce, optional

6 to 8 servings

Heat oven to 350°. Add flour to large (14 × 20-inch) oven cooking bag; shake to distribute. Place bag in roasting pan. Pour wine into bag; stir with plastic or wooden spoon to blend into flour. Set aside.

In small mixing bowl, mix rosemary, marjoram, salt, and pepper. Rub herb mixture evenly over meat. Place meat in cooking bag with flour. Add carrots, onions, and bay leaves to cooking bag. Close bag with provided nylon tie. Make six ½-inch slits in top of bag. Roast until meat is tender, 1½ to 2½ hours. Remove meat to heated platter. With slotted spoon, transfer vegetables to platter. Keep warm. Discard bay leaves. Pour juices into small saucepan. In 1-cup measure, blend cornstarch into water. Stir half of cornstarch mixture into juices. Heat to boiling, stirring constantly. Cook, stirring constantly, until thickened and bubbly. Blend in additional cornstarch if thicker gravy is desired; cook and stir until thickened and bubbly. Stir in bouquet sauce. Serve gravy with meat and vegetables.

Big Game Belgium

Slow braising tenderizes the shoulder roast in this recipe. You may substitute any big-game roast for the elk shoulder. Serve roast with buttered noodles.

½ cup all-purpose flour
2 teaspoons dried thyme leaves
¼ teaspoon salt
½ teaspoon pepper
3 pound elk shoulder roast, about 2 inches thick
3 tablespoons olive oil or vegetable oil
½ pound salt pork, diced
3 tablespoons butter or margarine
3 medium onions, thinly sliced
1 tablespoon granulated sugar
1 bottle (12 ounces) dark beer
2 tablespoons packed brown sugar
1 tablespoon snipped fresh parsley

4 to 6 servings

Heat oven to 325°. In large plastic food-storage bag, combine flour, thyme, salt, and pepper; shake to mix. Add meat; shake to coat. In Dutch oven, brown meat in oil over medium heat. Remove meat; set aside. Add salt pork to Dutch oven. Cook over medium heat, stirring frequently, until salt pork is crisp and golden brown. With slotted spoon, transfer salt pork to small mixing bowl; set aside. Melt butter in Dutch oven. Add onions. Cook and stir over medium heat until tender. Add granulated sugar. Cook and stir until onions are brown, about 10 minutes. Add beer and brown sugar. Stir, scraping bottom of pan to loosen browned bits. Return meat to Dutch oven. Add reserved salt pork. Cover; bake until meat is tender, about 2 hours. Transfer meat to platter. Garnish with parsley. Serve with pan juices if desired.

Venison Sauerbraten ◆ LOW-FAT

Marinating tenderizes and adds flavor to this roast. Use a shoulder roast, bottom round, or rump roast. Serve with hot buttered noodles and sliced apples.

MARINADE:

  6 cups water
  1 large onion, sliced
  2 teaspoons salt
10 whole black peppercorns
10 whole juniper berries, optional
  6 whole cloves
  1 bay leaf
 ½ cup vinegar

3½ to 4-pound deer, elk, or moose roast
  2 tablespoons vegetable oil
  1 medium red or green cabbage (about 2½ pounds), cut into 8 wedges
15 gingersnaps, finely crushed
  2 teaspoons sugar

6 to 8 servings

In large saucepan, combine all marinade ingredients except vinegar. Heat to boiling. Add vinegar. Cool slightly. Place roast in large glass or ceramic mixing bowl. Pour cooled marinade over roast. Cover tightly with plastic wrap. Refrigerate 2 to 3 days, turning meat once or twice.

Remove roast from marinade, reserving marinade. In Dutch oven, brown roast on all sides in oil over medium heat. Add marinade. Reduce heat; cover. Cook over low heat until tender, 2 to 3 hours. Heat oven to 175° just before meat is tender. With slotted spoon, transfer roast to oven-proof serving platter. Keep warm in oven.

Strain cooking liquid into 2-quart measure. Add water if necessary to equal 5 cups. Return liquid to Dutch oven. Heat to boiling. Add cabbage wedges. Return to boiling. Reduce heat; cover. Simmer until cabbage is tender, 15 to 20 minutes. With slotted spoon, transfer cabbage to platter with meat. In small bowl, combine crushed gingersnaps and sugar. Stir into liquid in Dutch oven. Cook over low heat, stirring occasionally, until bubbly and slightly thickened. Serve gingersnap sauce with roast and cabbage wedges.

Bear Stew ↑

Although any big-game meat can be used in this recipe, bear meat is particularly good.

1½ to 2 pounds bear stew meat
 ¼ cup all-purpose flour
 1 teaspoon dried marjoram leaves
 1 teaspoon salt
 ⅛ teaspoon pepper
 2 tablespoons vegetable oil
 1 can (16 ounces) whole tomatoes, undrained
 1 cup water
 ¼ cup white wine or water
 1 tablespoon vinegar
 1 medium onion, cut in half lengthwise and
    thinly sliced
 ½ cup chopped celery
 2 cloves garlic, minced
 1 bay leaf
 2 medium baking potatoes

4 to 6 servings

Remove all fat and silverskin from meat. Cut into 1-inch pieces. In large plastic food-storage bag, combine flour, marjoram, salt, and pepper; shake to mix. Add meat; shake to coat. In heavy medium saucepan, heat oil over medium-high heat until hot. Add meat and flour mixture. Brown, stirring occasionally. Add remaining ingredients except potatoes; mix well. Heat to boiling. Reduce heat; cover. Simmer 1 hour, stirring occasionally.

Cut potatoes into 1-inch chunks. Add to saucepan. Heat to boiling. Reduce heat; cover. Simmer until meat and potatoes are tender, about 1 hour, stirring occasionally. Discard bay leaf before serving.

Big Game and Onion Casserole Braised in Beer ◆ LOW-FAT

Serve this casserole with hot buttered egg noodles, a tossed salad, and colorful vegetables.

SPICE PACKET:
 7 sprigs fresh parsley
 1 bay leaf
 ½ teaspoon dried thyme leaves
 2 whole black peppercorns
 2 whole juniper berries

 2 pounds lean big-game pieces
 2 tablespoons butter or margarine, divided
 2 tablespoons olive oil or vegetable oil, divided
 3 medium onions, sliced
 2 cloves garlic, minced
 2 cups beer
 ⅔ cup venison stock (page 144) or beef broth
 1 tablespoon plus 2 teaspoons packed
    brown sugar
 ¾ teaspoon salt
 ¼ teaspoon pepper
 2 tablespoons cornstarch
 2 tablespoons red wine vinegar

6 to 8 servings

Heat oven to 300°. Place spice-packet ingredients on a 6-inch-square piece of double-thickness cheesecloth. Gather corners; tie closed with kitchen string. Set aside. Remove all fat and silverskin from meat. Cut into pieces about 2 × 3 inches across and ½ inch thick. In large skillet, melt 1 tablespoon butter in 1 tablespoon oil over medium-low heat. Brown meat on both sides over medium-high heat. With slotted spoon, transfer meat to medium mixing bowl or plate; set aside. In same skillet, melt remaining 1 tablespoon butter in 1 tablespoon oil over medium heat. Add onions and garlic. Cook and stir until onions are tender. Remove from heat.

In 3-quart casserole, place one-half of the meat. Top with one-half of the onions. Repeat with remaining meat and onions. Add cheesecloth-wrapped spice packet to casserole. In small mixing bowl, blend beer, stock, brown sugar, salt, and pepper. Pour over casserole ingredients. Cover. Bake until meat is tender, about 2 hours. Remove and discard spice packet.

In small bowl, blend cornstarch and vinegar. Pour into casserole. Stir to blend. Bake uncovered until thickened, about 30 minutes.

Elk Tenderloin Sauté ↑

You may substitute moose tenderloin, or deer or antelope loin, for the elk tenderloin in this recipe.

    2 cups water
    1 teaspoon salt
   ½ pound fresh pearl onions (about 1⅓ cups)
   ¼ cup all-purpose flour
   ½ teaspoon salt
   ¼ teaspoon pepper
 1½ pounds elk tenderloin, thinly sliced
    2 tablespoons butter or margarine
    2 tablespoons vegetable oil
 1¾ cups venison stock (page 144) or beef broth
    1 can (16 ounces) whole tomatoes, cut up
        and drained
   ½ cup burgundy
   ¼ cup tomato paste
    1 teaspoon Worcestershire sauce
   ¼ teaspoon dried thyme leaves
    1 or 2 cloves garlic, minced
    2 bay leaves
   ½ pound fresh mushrooms, cut into halves
        Hot cooked rice or noodles

4 to 6 servings

In small saucepan, heat water and 1 teaspoon salt to boiling. Add onions. Return to boiling. Reduce heat; cover. Simmer until onions are just tender, about 15 minutes. Drain and rinse under cold water. Set aside.

In large plastic food-storage bag, combine flour, ½ teaspoon salt, and the pepper; shake to mix. Add elk slices; shake to coat. In large skillet, melt butter in oil over medium heat. Add elk slices. Cook over medium-high heat until browned but still rare, stirring occasionally. Remove with slotted spoon; set aside. Add remaining ingredients except mushrooms and rice to cooking liquid in skillet; mix well. Add mushrooms and reserved onions. Heat to boiling. Reduce heat; cover. Simmer 10 minutes. Stir in elk slices. Cook, uncovered, over medium-low heat until slightly thickened, about 5 minutes. Discard bay leaves before serving. Serve over rice.

Venison Stroganoff

 1½ to 2 pounds deer, antelope, elk, or
        moose steaks
    2 tablespoons all-purpose flour
   ¾ teaspoon salt
    2 tablespoons butter or margarine
    2 cups sliced fresh mushrooms
    1 cup chopped onion
    2 cloves garlic, minced
   ¼ cup all-purpose flour
 1¾ cups venison stock (page 144) or beef broth
    3 tablespoons sherry
    2 tablespoons tomato paste
 1½ to 2 cups dairy sour cream
        Hot cooked noodles or rice

6 to 8 servings

Remove all fat and silverskin from steaks. Cut into thin strips. In large plastic food-storage bag, combine 2 tablespoons flour and the salt; shake to mix. Add venison strips; shake to coat. In large skillet, melt butter over low heat. Add venison strips. Cook over medium-high heat until browned, stirring constantly. Remove meat with slotted spoon; set aside. Add mushrooms, onion, and garlic to cooking liquid in skillet. Cook and stir over medium heat until onions are just tender. Stir in ¼ cup flour. Blend in stock, sherry, and tomato paste. Heat until bubbly, stirring constantly. Stir in sour cream and venison strips. Heat until just hot; do not boil. Serve over noodles.

Oven-Method Venison Jerky ◆ LOW-FAT

Follow recipe on page 152 for Traditional Venison Jerky, except prepare in oven rather than cold smoker. Jerky will not have smoke flavor. Heat oven to 150°. Prepare meat strips as directed. Place in single layer on cookie-cooling racks (fine-mesh or closely spaced bars work best). Cook meat until dry but not brittle, 4 to 5 hours, rearranging racks once. Use an oven thermometer to be sure oven does not get too warm. Refrigerate jerky for storage.

Venison and Beans ↑

A great dish to take to a pot-luck supper.

 6 slices bacon, chopped
1½ pounds deer, antelope, elk, or moose burger
 1 medium onion, chopped
 1 can (16 ounces) pork and beans
 1 can (16 ounces) kidney beans, drained
 1 can (16 ounces) butter beans or Great
   Northern beans, drained
 ⅓ cup packed brown sugar
 1 cup catsup
 2 tablespoons vinegar
 1 tablespoon Worcestershire sauce
 ½ teaspoon salt
 ¼ teaspoon prepared mustard

8 to 10 servings

Heat oven to 350°. In Dutch oven, cook bacon over medium-low heat, stirring occasionally, until crisp. Remove with slotted spoon; set aside. Drain all but 1 tablespoon bacon fat from Dutch oven. Add meat and onion. Cook over medium heat, stirring occasionally, until meat is no longer pink and onion is tender. Add reserved bacon and remaining ingredients to Dutch oven; mix well. Cover and bake until bubbly around edges, about 45 minutes.

Texas-Style Venison Chili  LOW-FAT

 1 to 1½ pounds boneless deer, moose, or elk
 ¼ cup all-purpose flour
 3 tablespoons bacon fat or vegetable oil
 2 medium onions, chopped
 3 to 5 cloves garlic, minced
 2 or 3 fresh green chilies, minced, or
   ½ to 1 teaspoon dried red pepper flakes
 3 cans (16 ounces) whole tomatoes, undrained
 1 teaspoon dried oregano leaves
 1 teaspoon dried basil leaves
 ½ teaspoon ground cumin
 1 medium green pepper, cut into ¾-inch chunks
   Hot cooked rice

6 to 8 servings

Trim meat if necessary; cut into ½-inch cubes. Place meat cubes and flour in large plastic food-storage bag; shake to coat. In Dutch oven, lightly brown meat in bacon fat over medium-high heat, stirring frequently. Add remaining ingredients except green pepper and rice. Heat to boiling over medium heat. Boil gently for 15 minutes. Reduce heat. Simmer for 1 to 1½ hours, stirring occasionally. Add green pepper. Simmer for 30 minutes longer. Serve over hot cooked rice.

Venison Meatloaf Supreme ↑

    2 pounds deer, antelope, elk, or moose burger
    2 cups soft bread crumbs
 1/2 cup venison stock (page 144) or beef broth
 1/2 cup chopped onion
    2 eggs, slightly beaten
    1 teaspoon salt
 1/2 teaspoon Worcestershire sauce
 1/4 teaspoon sugar
 1/4 teaspoon celery salt
 1/4 teaspoon dried crushed sage leaves
 1/4 teaspoon dried oregano leaves
 1/4 teaspoon pepper
    2 small tomatoes, peeled, halved, and seeded

6 to 8 servings

Heat oven to 325°. Grease 9 × 5-inch loaf pan; set aside. In large mixing bowl, combine all ingredients except tomatoes; mix well. Pat half of meat mixture into prepared pan. Arrange tomatoes on meat mixture, leaving 1/2 inch around edges of pan. Spread remaining meat mixture over tomatoes, pressing well around edges to seal. Bake until well browned, about 1 1/2 hours. Let stand 10 minutes. Remove to serving platter.

Big Game Goulash

    2 cups uncooked egg noodles
    1 pound lean ground big game
 1/2 cup chopped onion
    1 clove garlic, minced
    2 tablespoons vegetable oil
    1 can (16 ounces) whole tomatoes, cut up,
        juice reserved
    1 can (16 ounces) kidney beans, drained
    1 can (8 ounces) tomato sauce
    1 can (16 ounces) sliced potatoes, drained
    1 teaspoon salt
    1 teaspoon dried basil leaves
 1/4 teaspoon pepper

6 to 8 servings

Heat oven to 350°. Grease a 2-quart casserole; set aside. Cook noodles according to package directions. Rinse and drain. Place in prepared 2-quart casserole; set aside.

In medium skillet, cook meat, onion, and garlic in oil over medium heat, stirring occasionally, until meat is no longer pink and onion is tender. Add meat mixture and remaining ingredients to noodles. Mix well; cover. Bake until hot and bubbly around edges, 35 to 45 minutes.

Mexican Chorizo Sausage ↑

Boldly flavored, this sausage can be used for tacos, chili, or tiny appetizer meatballs.

2 pounds trimmed deer or other big-game meat
2 pounds boneless fatty pork shoulder or
   pork butt
2 tablespoons paprika
1 tablespoon salt
1 tablespoon black pepper
2 teaspoons crushed red pepper flakes
1 teaspoon sugar
1 teaspoon garlic powder
½ teaspoon dried oregano leaves
¼ teaspoon cumin seed
¼ cup white vinegar

About 4 pounds

Cut deer and pork into ¾-inch cubes. Place in large mixing bowl. In small bowl, mix remaining ingredients except vinegar. Sprinkle over meat; mix well. Chop or grind to medium consistency. Return meat mixture to large mixing bowl. Add vinegar; mix well. Cover bowl tightly with plastic wrap. Refrigerate for at least one hour to blend flavors. Cook over medium heat, stirring occasionally, until brown; use for tacos or chili. Or, shape into tiny meatballs or patties, and fry over medium heat until browned and cooked through, turning to brown all sides. Sausage can also be frozen uncooked.

Garlic Sausage

Serve patties of Garlic Sausage as a main course with a hearty soup, tossed salad, and French bread. This sausage is also excellent on pizzas or in chili.

1½ pounds boneless fatty pork shoulder or
   pork butt
1 pound trimmed deer or other big-game meat
3 to 4 teaspoons fresh minced garlic
1 tablespoon salt
1 teaspoon pepper
½ cup water

About 3 pounds

Cut pork and deer into ¾-inch cubes. Place in large mixing bowl. Sprinkle garlic, salt, and pepper over meat; mix well. Chop or grind to medium consistency. Return meat mixture to large mixing bowl. Add water; mix well. Cover bowl tightly with plastic wrap. Refrigerate for two days to blend flavors and allow garlic to mellow. Shape into thin patties and fry over medium heat until browned and cooked through, turning once. Sausage can also be frozen uncooked after two-day blending period.

Venison Breakfast Sausage  FAST

1 pound trimmed deer or other big-game meat
6 ounces lean bacon ends or slab bacon
¾ teaspoon salt
1 teaspoon dried crushed sage leaves
½ teaspoon ground ginger
¼ teaspoon pepper

1½ pounds

Cut the deer and bacon into ¾-inch cubes. Place in medium mixing bowl. In small bowl, mix salt, sage, ginger, and pepper. Sprinkle over meat; mix well. Chop or grind to desired consistency. Shape into thin patties and fry over medium heat until browned and cooked through, turning once. Sausage can also be frozen uncooked.

Potato Sausage ◆ LOW-FAT

Fry this sausage in patties for breakfast, brunch, or dinner, or use it to make an interesting meatloaf.

1 quart water
2 pounds peeled red potatoes
1 pound trimmed deer, antelope, elk, or moose
1 pound boneless fatty pork shoulder or
   pork butt
1 medium onion, coarsely chopped
1 egg, beaten
1 tablespoon salt
½ teaspoon ground allspice
¼ teaspoon dried ground sage leaves
¼ teaspoon dried basil leaves
¼ teaspoon sugar

4 pounds

In 2-quart saucepan, heat water to boiling. Add potatoes. Return to boiling. Reduce heat; cover. Simmer until potatoes are fork-tender, 25 to 35 minutes. Drain. Cool potatoes; cut into ¾-inch cubes.

Cut deer and pork into ¾-inch cubes. In large mixing bowl, combine deer, pork, potato cubes, onion, and egg. In small bowl, mix remaining ingredients. Sprinkle over meat and potato mixture; mix well. Cover bowl tightly with plastic wrap. Refrigerate at least 1 hour to blend flavors.

Chop or grind meat and potato mixture to medium consistency. Shape into thin patties. Fry in non-stick skillet over medium-low heat in a small amount of vegetable oil until browned and cooked through, turning once.

Dressing Small Game

Proper field care of small game ensures excellent eating. Field-dress rabbits, hares, and squirrels as soon as possible, or the delicately flavored meat may pick up an unpleasant taste. Squirrel seems particularly susceptible to off-tastes, so knowledgeable hunters take time to field-dress squirrels immediately after shooting. Most raccoon hunters skin and dress their raccoons at home shortly after the hunt. Raccoon meat doesn't suffer from the minor delay, and the pelt is more valuable if it hasn't been cut for field-dressing.

A great deal has been written about small game transmitting diseases to humans. Such diseases are contracted by handling entrails or uncooked meat from infected animals. Bacteria passes through cuts in a person's skin or through the mucous membranes. But infected animals are rarely encountered, because the diseases usually kill them or weaken them so much that predators can easily capture them.

To avoid any danger, never shoot an animal that moves erratically or otherwise appears sick. Wear rubber gloves when dressing or skinning any small game. Never touch your mouth or eyes, and wash your hands thoroughly when finished. Dispose of the entrails and skin in a spot where dogs and cats can't reach them and become infected. For safer disposal, some hunters carry plastic bags.

When field-dressing small game, you may encounter various internal parasites. Most of these, while visually unappealing, do not harm the meat and are removed during dressing or skinning.

Raccoon populations in some areas of the country carry a roundworm that may be found in the droppings and on the pelt. In very rare circumstances, this parasite can be transmitted to humans. Although the possibility of contamination is slim, raccoon hunters should wear rubber gloves while dressing and skinning.

When handling rabbits, wear the gloves not only for dressing and skinning, but also during all stages of kitchen preparation. Rabbits occasionally carry *tularemia,* a bacterial disease that can be transmitted to humans. Thorough cooking destroys the bacteria.

After dressing, small-game animals must be cooled properly. Don't put them in a hot car or carry them for hours in the pocket of your hunting coat. Instead, leave them in a shaded spot, out of the reach of predators. Some hunters hang their field-dressed animals in a shady tree, so the carcasses can drain as well as cool. Never put an animal in a plastic bag until it's completely cooled.

In warm weather, it's best to chill the dressed animals in a cooler. Reusable plastic ice packs are better than plain ice, since they won't fill the cooler with melted water. Plastic pop bottles filled with water and then frozen work well also.

Before skinning, try to determine the animal's age, because this may affect the way you cook it. The tail of a young squirrel tapers to a point, while the tail of an old one is the same width throughout. A young rabbit has soft, flexible ears and a small cleft in the upper lip; an old one has stiffer ears, often with white edges, and a deeply cleft upper lip. In all kinds of small game, the meat of old animals is darker in color. Also, the teeth darken and dull with age, and the claws become blunt.

How to Field-dress Small Game

EQUIPMENT for field-dressing small game includes (1) hunting knife, (2) rubber gloves, (3) plastic bags, (4) paper towels, (5) cord for hanging dressed animals in a tree.

MAKE a shallow cut (dotted line) from the vent to the rib cage. Be sure not to puncture the intestines. Some hunters extend the cut through the rib cage to the neck.

PULL OUT all the entrails. Check a rabbit's liver for white spots indicating disease; if it's clean, save it in a plastic bag with the heart. Wipe cavity with paper towels.

How to Skin a Rabbit or Hare

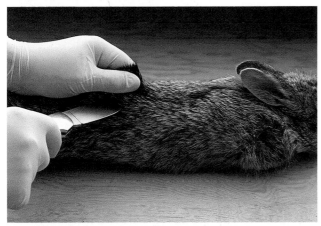

PINCH the hide up and away from the middle of the rabbit's spine. Slit the hide from the spine down the sides, being careful not to cut the meat.

GRASP the hide with both hands and pull in opposite directions. Keep pulling until all the legs are skinned up to the feet.

CUT off the head, feet, and tail. If you did not field-dress the rabbit before skinning, slit the underside from vent to neck, then remove all internal organs. Save liver and heart if desired.

CLEAN body cavity, removing any material left after dressing. Rinse briefly under running water and pat dry. Squirrels can also be skinned this way, but not as easily (see page 28 for an easier squirrel-skinning method).

CUT through the base of the tailbone, starting on the underside of the tail. Stop when the bone is severed; do not cut the skin on the top side of the tail.

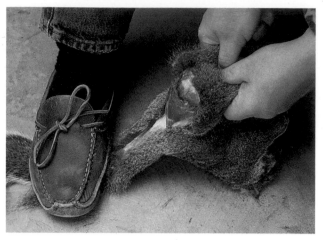

PLACE the squirrel on the ground, and set your foot on the base of the tail. Pull up on the rear legs, peeling the skin all the way to the front legs.

PEEL the "britches" off the rear legs to the ankle joints. Keep your foot firmly on the base of the tail until all skinning is complete.

REMOVE the squirrel's back feet by cutting through the ankle joints with a knife or game shears. If using a knife, cut away from yourself as pictured.

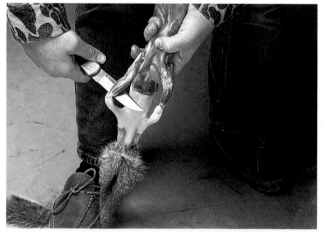

PULL each front leg out of the skin, as far as the wrist joint. Use the fingers of your free hand to help loosen the skin at the elbow. Then cut each front foot off at the wrist joint (pictured).

CUT the head off. Remove any glands and clean out the body cavity as described in the rabbit-skinning sequence on page 27. Several long hairs usually remain on the wrists; cut these off with your knife or shears.

HANG the raccoon by the rear legs, and cut the skin around the rear feet. The raccoon in this picture is hanging from a special raccoon-skinning gambrel.

CUT along the inside of each rear leg to the base of the tail. Peel the pelt back to the base of the tail. Begin peeling the skin off the abdomen.

USE your knife as shown to skin the pelt from the spine above the tail. Cut through the tailbone close to the rump. Leave the tailbone inside the pelt.

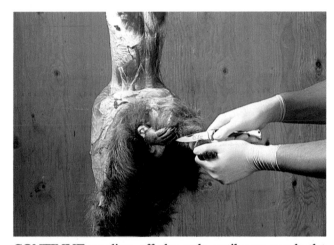

CONTINUE peeling off the pelt until you reach the shoulders, using your knife only when necessary. Cut the skin around the front feet (pictured).

PULL the pelt off the front legs and then off the head, cutting carefully at the eyes and rear base of the ears. Cut the pelt off at the nose. Turn it right-side-out to dry. Cut and peel the tail skin to remove the bone.

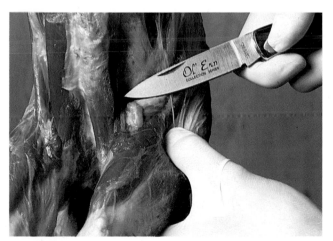

REMOVE the glands that lie under the front legs and above the base of the tail. Cut off the head and feet. Slit the abdomen from vent to neck. Remove the internal organs, rinse the raccoon, and pat it dry.

47

Portioning Small Game

Small game is usually cut into serving pieces before it is cooked or frozen. Pieces are more convenient to freeze than a whole carcass, because they can be arranged into a compact bundle with few air spaces.

The portioning method shown below works with squirrels, rabbits, hares, and raccoons. The rear legs are the meatiest pieces, followed by the *saddle* or loin portion, then the front legs. The ribs contain very little meat, but can be used for making stock.

Game shears are an excellent tool for cutting up squirrels, rabbits, and hares. You may need a heavy knife, however, to cut through the thick backbone of a raccoon.

Wear rubber gloves when handling raw rabbit or hare. In some locations raccoons may carry encephalitis in early fall, so gloves are a good precaution when portioning raccoons taken at that time.

How to Cut Up Small Game (pictured: Rabbit)

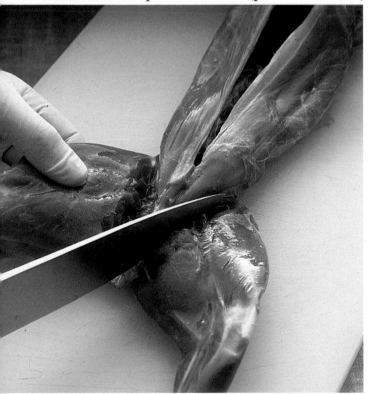

PLACE the animal on its back on a cutting board. Cut into the rear leg at a point near the backbone. When you come to the leg bone, stop cutting. If using a game shears, snip the meat around the bone.

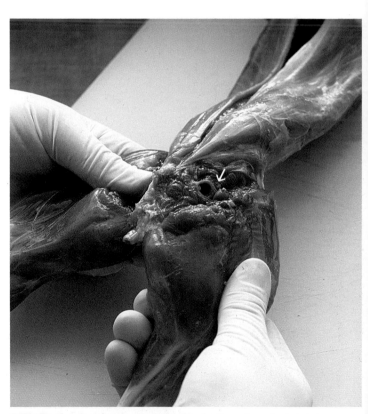

BEND the leg back to pop the ball-and-socket joint (arrow). Cut through the joint to remove the leg. Repeat with the other leg. On a large rabbit, hare, or raccoon, each rear leg can be split in two at the knee.

48

A Simple Method for Cutting Up a Squirrel

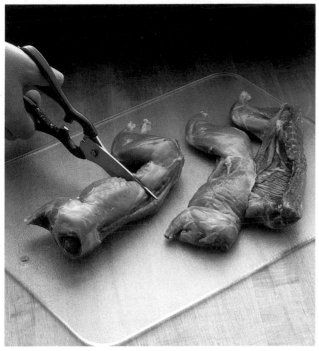

CUT the squirrel in half behind the ribs (left), or along the backbone (right). If the squirrel is small, no further cutting will be necessary.

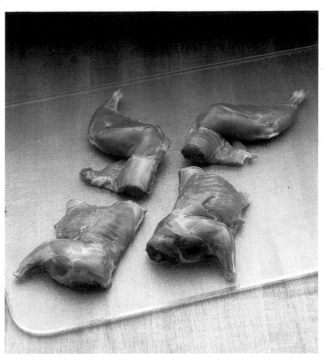

QUARTER a large squirrel by cutting each half apart. Quartered squirrels are easier to fry than halved ones, and look more attractive when served.

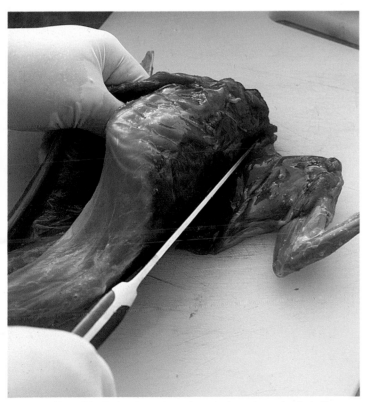

REMOVE the front legs by cutting close to the rib cage and behind the shoulder blades. The legs come off easier this way because you don't cut through joints. On a large animal, cut each leg in two at the elbow.

CUT the back into two or three pieces, depending on the animal's size. Remove the rib cage, if desired. When portioning a raccoon or large hare, you can also split the back along the spine, making four to six pieces.

Sherried Squirrel or Rabbit ↑

4 squirrels or 2 wild rabbits, cut up
2 quarts water
1 tablespoon salt
2 teaspoons vinegar
⅓ cup all-purpose flour
1 teaspoon salt
⅛ teaspoon pepper
2 tablespoons butter or margarine
2 tablespoons vegetable oil
8 ounces fresh whole mushrooms

SHERRY SAUCE:
1 cup rabbit stock (page 145) or chicken broth
¼ cup sherry
1 tablespoon Worcestershire sauce
¼ teaspoon seasoned salt
2 or 3 drops hot red pepper sauce

4 to 6 servings

In large glass or ceramic bowl, combine squirrel pieces, water, 1 tablespoon salt, and the vinegar. Cover bowl with plastic wrap. Let stand at room temperature 1 hour. Drain, discarding liquid. Pat squirrel pieces dry; set aside.

Heat oven to 350°. In large plastic food-storage bag, combine flour, 1 teaspoon salt, and the pepper; shake to mix. Add squirrel pieces; shake to coat. In large skillet, melt butter in oil over medium-low heat. Add squirrel pieces; brown on all sides over medium-high heat. Transfer squirrel pieces and drippings to 3-quart casserole. Add mushrooms. In 2-cup measure, combine all sherry sauce ingredients. Pour over squirrel pieces and mushrooms. Cover casserole. Bake until tender, about 1½ hours.

Southern Fried Squirrel or Rabbit with Gravy

⅓ cup all-purpose flour
½ teaspoon salt
⅛ teaspoon black pepper
⅛ teaspoon cayenne pepper, optional
2 squirrels or 1 wild rabbit, cut up
   Vegetable oil
3 tablespoons all-purpose flour
1½ cups milk or chicken broth
   Salt and pepper
   Brown bouquet sauce, optional

2 or 3 servings

In large plastic food-storage bag, combine ⅓ cup flour, the salt, black pepper, and cayenne pepper; shake to mix. Add squirrel pieces; shake to coat. In large skillet, heat ⅛ inch oil for squirrel, or ¼ inch oil for rabbit, over medium-high heat until hot. Add coated meat; brown on all sides. Reduce heat; cover tightly. Cook over very low heat until tender, 35 to 45 minutes for squirrel, 20 to 25 minutes for rabbit, turning pieces once. Remove cover; cook 5 minutes longer to crisp. Transfer meat to plate lined with paper towels. Set aside and keep warm.

Discard all but 3 tablespoons oil. Over medium heat, stir flour into reserved oil. Blend in milk. Cook over medium heat, stirring constantly, until thickened and bubbly. Add salt and pepper to taste. Add bouquet sauce if darker color is desired. Serve gravy with meat.

Cranberry Braised Raccoon

2½ to 3 pounds raccoon pieces, fat and
  glands removed
1 cup finely chopped cranberries
1 cup apple cider
¼ cup honey
1 teaspoon grated orange peel
¾ teaspoon salt
⅛ teaspoon ground cloves
⅛ teaspoon ground nutmeg

3 or 4 servings

Place raccoon pieces in large saucepan. In small
mixing bowl, combine remaining ingredients; mix
well. Pour over raccoon pieces. Heat to boiling.
Reduce heat; cover. Simmer until raccoon is tender,
2 to 3 hours, stirring once or twice.

Cranberry Raccoon in Crockpot

Follow recipe above, using crockpot instead of
saucepan. Cover and cook on low heat until raccoon
is tender, 9 to 10 hours.

← Hasenpfeffer

*Marinating tenderizes hare or mature rabbits in this classic
German recipe. Serve with hot buttered egg noodles,
braised red cabbage, rye bread, and a good beer.*

1 hare or 2 wild rabbits, cut up

MARINADE:
2 cups red wine
1 cup water
½ cup cider vinegar
2 cloves garlic, minced
½ teaspoon dried thyme leaves
½ teaspoon dried rosemary leaves
½ teaspoon dried marjoram leaves
10 whole black peppercorns

½ cup all-purpose flour
6 slices bacon, cut up
8 ounces fresh mushrooms, cut into quarters
1 cup chopped onion
1 to 3 tablespoons butter
1 teaspoon salt
½ cup dairy sour cream

4 to 6 servings

In large glass or ceramic mixing bowl, combine hare
pieces and all marinade ingredients. Cover bowl
with plastic wrap. Refrigerate for 2 or 3 days, turning hare pieces daily.

Lift hare pieces out of marinade. Pat dry with paper
towels; set aside. Strain and reserve 1½ cups marinade, discarding herbs and excess marinade. Place
flour on a sheet of waxed paper. Add hare pieces,
turning to coat. In Dutch oven, cook bacon over
medium heat until almost crisp. Add mushrooms
and onion. Cook until onion is tender, stirring
occasionally. Remove vegetable mixture with slotted spoon; set aside. Add 1 tablespoon butter to
pan. Add hare pieces. Brown on all sides, adding
additional butter if necessary. Return vegetable
mixture to Dutch oven. Add salt and reserved marinade. Heat to boiling. Reduce heat; cover. Simmer
until hare pieces are tender, 1 to 1¼ hours. With
slotted spoon, transfer hare pieces to heated serving
platter. Set aside and keep warm. Blend sour cream
into cooking liquid. Cook over medium heat until
heated through, stirring occasionally; do not boil.
Serve sauce over hare.

Coonpfeffer

Follow recipe above, substituting 3 to 3½ pounds
raccoon pieces for the hare. Combine raccoon
pieces and marinade. Refrigerate for 3 to 4 days.
Continue as directed above, increasing cooking time
to 1½ to 2 hours.

Raccoon with Sauerkraut →

1 tablespoon all-purpose flour
1 can (16 ounces) sauerkraut, rinsed and drained
1 large tart apple, cored and chopped
½ cup chicken broth
¼ cup packed brown sugar
½ teaspoon caraway seed
1 bay leaf
2 tablespoons Worcestershire sauce
½ teaspoon salt
½ teaspoon paprika
⅛ teaspoon pepper
3 to 4 pounds raccoon pieces, fat and glands removed
3 medium baking potatoes, cut in half

4 or 5 servings

Heat oven to 350°. Add flour to large (14 × 20-inch) oven cooking bag; shake to distribute. Place bag in 2-inch-deep roasting pan; set aside. In medium mixing bowl, combine sauerkraut, apple, chicken broth, brown sugar, and caraway seed; mix well. Spoon into cooking bag. Add bay leaf. In small bowl, combine Worcestershire sauce, salt, paprika, and pepper. Brush over raccoon pieces. Arrange raccoon pieces over sauerkraut mixture. Add potato halves. Close cooking bag with provided nylon tie. Make six ½-inch slits in top of bag. Bake until raccoon pieces are tender, 2 to 3 hours. Discard bay leaf before serving.

Tuscan Hare with Pasta

Hare is highly favored by Europeans. Many little restaurants in the Tuscany region of Italy serve hare sauce over pasta or polenta (cornmeal mush) during hunting season.

1 hare, cut up
3 stalks celery, cut into 2-inch pieces
3 carrots, cut into 2-inch pieces
½ teaspoon dried rosemary leaves
1 bay leaf
10 whole black peppercorns
2 tablespoons red wine vinegar
3 cups dry red wine
2 cups water
⅓ cup olive oil
1 large onion, chopped
2 cloves garlic, minced
1 can (16 ounces) whole tomatoes, undrained
¼ cup tomato paste
2 teaspoons salt
Hot cooked linguini or wide egg noodles
Grated Parmesan cheese

4 to 6 servings

In Dutch oven, combine hare pieces, celery, carrots, rosemary, bay leaf, peppercorns, vinegar, wine, and water. Heat to boiling. Reduce heat; cover. Simmer for 45 minutes. Remove cover. Cook over medium heat for 1½ hours longer. Remove hare pieces; set aside to cool slightly. Strain cooking liquid into 2-cup measure; discard vegetables. If there is more than 1 cup cooking liquid, boil in medium saucepan until reduced to 1 cup. If there is less than 1 cup cooking liquid, add water to equal 1 cup. Set cooking liquid aside. Remove hare meat from bones; discard bones. Shred meat coarsely with fingers.

In Dutch oven, heat oil over medium heat. Add shredded meat. Cook, stirring frequently, until meat begins to brown, about 5 minutes. Scrape browned bits from bottom of pan. Add onion and garlic; cook 10 minutes longer. Add reserved cooking liquid, tomatoes and juice, tomato paste, and salt. Heat to boiling. Reduce heat to medium. Cook until moderately thick, 30 to 45 minutes, stirring occasionally. Serve sauce over hot linguini; sprinkle with grated Parmesan cheese.

Spanish Rabbit →

- 3 tablespoons olive oil
- 1 wild rabbit, cut up
- 2 medium onions, chopped
- 1 green pepper, cut into ½-inch pieces
- 2 cloves garlic, minced
- 2 cups rabbit stock (page 145) or chicken broth
- 1 cup uncooked long grain rice
- ½ cup snipped fresh parsley
- ¼ teaspoon salt
- ¼ teaspoon crushed saffron threads
- ¼ teaspoon pepper
- 2 medium tomatoes, seeded, chopped, and drained
- 1 cup large pitted black olives
- 1 jar (2 ounces) diced pimiento, drained

2 or 3 servings

In Dutch oven, heat oil over medium heat. Add rabbit pieces. Fry 10 minutes, turning pieces over once. Remove with slotted spoon; set aside. Add onions, green pepper, and garlic to oil. Cook and stir until tender. Add rabbit pieces, stock, rice, parsley, salt, saffron, and pepper. Heat to boiling. Reduce heat; cover. Simmer until rice is tender and liquid is absorbed, 45 to 55 minutes. Stir in tomatoes, olives, and pimiento. Re-cover. Cook until heated through, about 5 minutes.

Tomato-Rabbit Casserole

- 1 tablespoon butter or margarine
- 1 tablespoon vegetable oil
- 1 wild rabbit, cut up
- 3 medium potatoes, quartered
- 4 to 6 small onions
- 1 can (16 ounces) whole tomatoes, undrained
- 1 cup vegetable juice cocktail
- 1 bay leaf
- ½ teaspoon salt
- ½ teaspoon dried basil leaves
- ¼ teaspoon dried tarragon leaves
- ¼ teaspoon pepper

2 or 3 servings

Heat oven to 350°. In medium skillet, melt butter in oil over medium-low heat. Add rabbit pieces; brown on all sides over medium-high heat. Transfer rabbit pieces to 3-quart casserole. Add remaining ingredients; mix well. Cover; bake until rabbit pieces are tender, about 1½ hours. Discard bay leaf before serving.

Dressing Upland Birds & Waterfowl

In warm weather, all birds should be gutted as soon as they're shot. In cool weather, gutting can wait until the end of the day's hunt.

Plucking the birds is seldom practical in the middle of a hunt. But if you do have the opportunity, you'll find the feathers pull out more easily then, while the birds are still warm. When plucking in the field, put the feathers in a bag instead of scattering them around. Be sure to check state laws on the transport of game birds. In many states, at least one wing must remain fully feathered and attached to the carcass.

When hunting in warm weather, keep a cooler filled with ice in your car or duck boat. Chill the dressed birds as soon as possible.

Before plucking or skinning any waterfowl, try to determine its age. Old birds may be tough unless cooked with moist heat. Young geese and ducks are smaller than old ones, and the plumage may not be fully colored. If you notice a lot of pinfeathers when plucking, the bird is probably young.

Most upland birds have short life spans, but turkeys and pheasants often live several years. Check the spurs on the legs of a tom turkey or rooster pheasant. Long, pointed spurs indicate an old bird; short, rounded spurs, a young one.

Birds, like big game, can be tenderized by aging. Dress the birds but leave the skin and feathers on; then store them, uncovered, in a refrigerator for a few days.

If possible, birds to be served whole should be plucked rather than skinned. The skin helps keep the meat moist. Waterfowl have thick, tough skin that doesn't tear easily, so they're easier to pluck than upland birds. An upland bird that's badly shot-up may have to be skinned, because the delicate skin would rip during plucking. Sage grouse, sea ducks, and fish-eating ducks like mergansers are usually skinned, because the skin of these birds is strongly flavored.

Skinning a bird saves time, but the meat may dry out in cooking. You can save even more time by using the breasting method shown on page 37, if you like pieces instead of a whole bird.

In rare instances, ducks have parasites in the breast meat, which show up as white, rice-like grains. Although safe to eat if thoroughly cooked, the meat is unappealing and is usually discarded.

How to Field-dress Birds (pictured: Pheasant)

EQUIPMENT for field-dressing upland birds and waterfowl includes (1) small hunting knife; (2) plastic bags, which can double as gloves; (3) paper towels.

CUT the skin from the vent toward the breastbone. Some hunters pluck the feathers between the vent and breastbone before cutting.

MAKE a short slit above the breast toward the chin. Pull out the windpipe. Remove the *crop,* a flexible sac that lies between the bird's breast and chin, and any undigested food it may contain.

REMOVE the entrails, including the lungs. If desired, save the heart, gizzard, and liver, storing them in a plastic bag. Be sure to trim the green gall sac from the liver. Wipe the inside of the bird with paper towels.

How to Skin a Bird (pictured: Pheasant)

CUT off the last two joints of the wing with game shears or a knife. Cut off the feet, removing the leg tendons from an upland bird (page 38) if desired.

PLACE fingers in the slit where the crop was removed during field-dressing; pull to skin breast and legs. If crop is still in, slit skin and remove crop first.

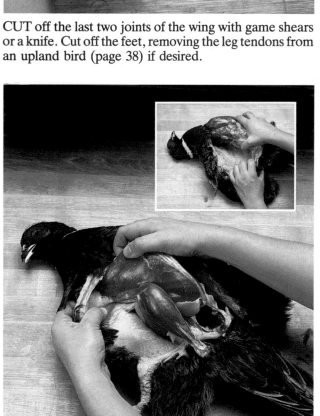

PULL the skin away from the wing joints, turning the skin inside-out over the joints as though peeling off a stocking. Free both wings, then peel the skin off the back of the bird (inset).

REMOVE the head and tail with game shears. If the bird wasn't dressed before skinning, pull out the windpipe and entrails. Clean the cavity thoroughly. Rinse the bird and pat it dry.

How to Breast a Bird to Retain the Legs (pictured: Pheasant)

CUT off the feet and pull the skin off the breast and legs as described in the skinning sequence on the opposite page. Do not skin the wings.

SLICE breast halves away from the breastbone, using a fillet knife. Keep the blade as close to the bone as possible. Cut the meat away from the wishbone to free completely.

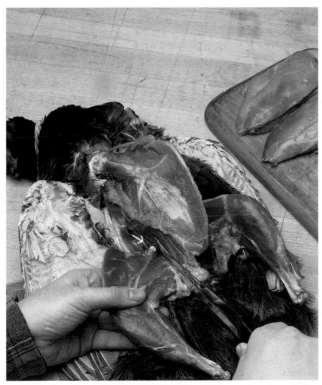

PUSH the leg down, popping the ball-and-socket joint (arrow). Cut through the joint to remove the leg. Remove other leg. If the bird wasn't field-dressed, remove liver, heart, and gizzard if you wish to save them.

CUT apart the thigh and drumstick if desired. Dispose of the carcass. With this method of breasting, the only meat discarded is on the back and wings. The boneless breast halves are easy to cook.

How to Wet-pluck a Bird (pictured: Chukar Partridge)

WET the bird thoroughly by holding it underneath a running faucet. If wet-plucking waterfowl, rub the breast with your thumb to ensure that the thick down feathers are saturated with water.

DIP the bird several times in simmering (160° to 180°F) water. For waterfowl, add a tablespoon of dish-washing liquid to help saturate the feathers. Rinse any soapy water from the cavity of a field-dressed bird.

RUB the body feathers with your thumb. They should strip off easily. If they don't, dip the bird in hot water again. Pull out the large feathers of the wing and tail, using a pliers if necessary.

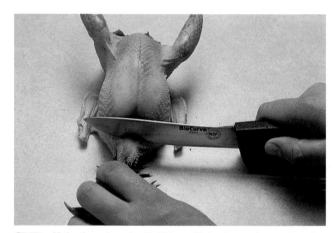

CUT off the head and tail. Slice off the feet, removing the leg tendons from upland birds (page 38) if desired. Clean the body cavity, and take out the windpipe if still present. Rinse the cavity, and pat the bird dry.

How to Dry-pluck a Bird (pictured: Bobwhite Quail)

GRASP only a few feathers at a time, and pull gently in the direction in which they grow. Pluck over a grocery bag to minimize the mess.

USE a pliers, if necessary, to pull out the wing and tail feathers. Some hunters cut off the outer two joints of the wings; little meat is lost.

SINGE any downy feathers or "hair" with a gas burner. Finish cleaning as described in the last step of the wet-plucking sequence shown above.

How to Wax Waterfowl (pictured: Mallard)

HEAT a large pot of water to a gentle boil. Melt several chunks of special duck-picking wax or paraffin in the water. The floating layer of melted wax should be at least ¼ inch thick.

ROUGH-PLUCK the larger feathers from the body, legs, wings, and tail. Pull only a few feathers at a time. Leave the smaller feathers on the bird, since they make the wax adhere better.

DIP the bird in the wax and water. Swish it around gently, then slowly remove it from the wax. Hold the bird up until the wax hardens enough that you can set it down on newspapers without sticking. Or, hang it by wedging the head between closely spaced nails on a board.

ALLOW the bird to cool until the wax is fairly hard. To speed the process, you can dip the bird in a bucket of cold water. Repeat the dipping and cooling until a layer of wax has built up at least ⅛ inch thick. Allow the wax to cool completely and harden.

PEEL the hardened wax off the bird. The feathers will come off with the wax, leaving the skin smooth. You can reuse the wax if you melt it again and strain it through cheesecloth to remove the feathers.

CUT off the head, feet, and tail. Remove the windpipe and entrails if the bird was not dressed before waxing. Remove wax from the cavity of a dressed bird. Clean the cavity thoroughly, rinse the bird, and pat it dry.

Portioning Upland Birds & Waterfowl

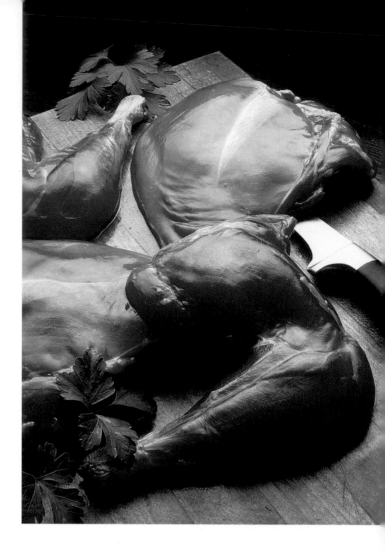

Whether to portion a bird, and how, depends mainly on its size and the cooking method. Any upland bird or waterfowl can be cooked whole. The larger ones, such as pheasant, turkey, mallard, and goose, can be cut into traditional pieces if preferred. Birds up to the size of a pheasant can also be split into halves.

If you portion a bird, skinning is optional. When you cut it up, save the backbone, neck, and any bones left from breasting. These parts make excellent stock (page 145). Most cooks do not make stock from small birds like doves, woodcock, and quail.

Breasting is quick and easy, and many hunters prefer it when they have a number of birds to process. The breasting method shown on page 37 saves not only the breast but also the thighs and drumsticks, so very little meat is wasted.

How to Split a Bird into Halves (pictured: Hungarian Partridge)

SPLIT the back by cutting along one side of the backbone with game shears. If desired, cut along the other side of the backbone and remove it.

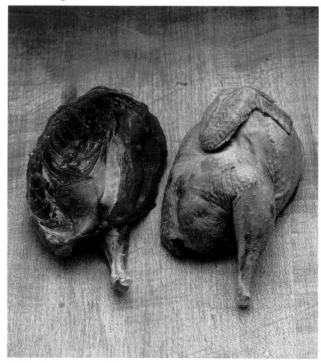

CUT along one side of the breastbone and through the wishbone. You can remove the breastbone by making a second cut along the other side of it.

How to Cut Up a Bird *(pictured: Pheasant)*

REMOVE the wings by cutting through the joint next to the breast. For another way of handling the wings, see the photo sequence of the French portioning technique on the opposite page.

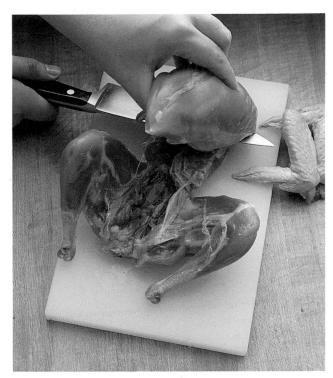

SEPARATE the breast from the back by cutting through the ribs. When you reach the shoulder, grasp the breast in one hand and the back in the other; bend the carcass as if it were hinged. Cut the breast and back apart.

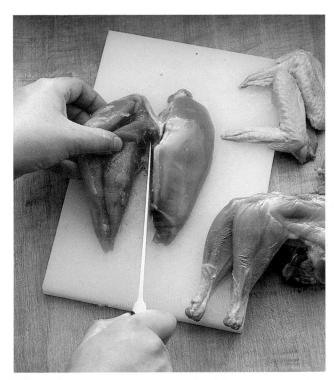

DIVIDE the breast into halves by cutting along one side of the breastbone, then cutting away the wishbone. You can also cut along the other side of the breastbone and remove it. Or, bone the breast as shown in the breasting sequence on page 37.

BEGIN cutting the leg away from the backbone, then bend it back to expose the ball-and-socket joint (arrow). Cut through the socket to remove the leg. If desired, separate the thigh from the drumstick by cutting through the knee joint.

Grilled Marinated Game Birds

2 whole pheasants or 4 whole partridge, skin on
1 recipe Lemon-Garlic Marinade (page 148) or
  other marinade
  Salt and freshly ground black pepper

4 servings

Split birds into halves with game shears (page 39). Place pheasant halves in large plastic food-storage bag. Pour prepared marinade over birds; seal bag. Refrigerate for at least 3 hours, or overnight, turning bag over occasionally.

Start charcoal briquets in grill. When briquets are covered with ash, spread them evenly in grill. Place grate above hot coals. Remove birds from marinade; reserve marinade. Arrange birds on grate, skin-side down. Grill until breasts are browned, 10 to 15 minutes, basting after every 5 minutes with reserved marinade. Turn birds over; continue grilling and basting until juices run clear when thigh is pricked. Remove from grill; season with salt and pepper.

← ## Roast Pheasant with Sauerkraut

The combination of sauerkraut and lingonberries makes this dish unusual, but delicious. Serve with crusty French bread and a good red wine.

1 whole pheasant, skin on
2 tablespoons butter, softened
2 slices bacon, cut up
1 can (16 ounces) sauerkraut, rinsed and
  drained
1 cup pheasant stock (page 145) or
  chicken broth
¼ cup cognac or brandy
1 cup pheasant stock or chicken broth
⅓ cup canned lingonberries, rinsed*
3 tablespoons butter or margarine

2 or 3 servings

Heat oven to 375°. Rub softened butter over pheasant. Place in small roasting pan; cover. Roast until pheasant is tender and juices run clear when thigh is pricked, 35 to 45 minutes.

While pheasant is roasting, begin preparing remaining ingredients. In medium skillet, cook bacon over low heat until lightly browned. Add sauerkraut and 1 cup pheasant stock. Cook over medium heat until most of the liquid evaporates, 12 to 15 minutes. Remove from heat; set aside and keep warm.

When pheasant is done, transfer from roaster to heated platter; set aside and keep warm. Pour drippings from roaster into small bowl; set aside. In small saucepan, heat cognac gently over low heat until warm. Remove from heat; carefully ignite with a long match. When flame dies, add 1 cup pheasant stock and the lingonberries. Cook over high heat until the liquid is reduced by half, 10 to 15 minutes. Skim fat from reserved drippings. Add drippings and 3 tablespoons butter to lingonberry mixture; cook, stirring occasionally, until butter melts, about 2 minutes. Serve lingonberry sauce with pheasant and sauerkraut.

*Variation: Substitute whole-berry cranberry sauce for lingonberries if you can't find lingonberries.

Broiled Marinated Game Birds

Follow recipe at left, cooking in preheated broiler instead of over charcoal. Arrange birds on broiler rack, skin-side down. Place rack 4 to 6 inches from heat. Broil until done, 20 to 35 minutes, turning once and basting several times.

Sharptail on Mushroom Toast →

Elegant fare for a small dinner party. This recipe works equally well with venison tenderloins.

- ¼ cup dry red wine
- ¼ cup grouse stock (page 145) or chicken broth
- 1½ teaspoons all-purpose flour
- ¼ teaspoon dry mustard
- ¼ teaspoon salt
- 4 tablespoons butter or margarine
- 4 slices French bread, ¾ inch thick and 5 to 6 inches across
- 1 tablespoon chopped shallot
- 1 tablespoon butter or margarine
- 8 ounces fresh mushrooms, very finely chopped
  Salt and freshly ground black pepper
- 1 tablespoon butter or margarine
- 1 tablespoon vegetable oil
- 4 boneless breast halves from 2 sharptail grouse
- 2 teaspoons snipped fresh parsley, optional

4 servings

In small bowl, blend wine, stock, flour, dry mustard, and ¼ teaspoon salt; set aside. In medium skillet, melt 2 tablespoons butter. Add 2 slices bread; turn quickly to coat both sides with melted butter. Cook over medium heat until golden brown on both sides. Repeat with remaining bread slices and 2 tablespoons butter; set aside and keep warm.

In medium skillet, cook and stir shallot in 1 tablespoon butter over medium heat until tender. Add chopped mushrooms. Cook over medium heat, stirring frequently, until the liquid has cooked off, about 10 minutes. Remove from heat. Salt and pepper to taste; set aside and keep warm.

In another medium skillet, melt remaining 1 tablespoon butter in oil over medium-low heat. Add breast halves. Cook over medium heat until well-browned on both sides but still moist in the center, about 10 minutes. Remove from skillet. Set aside and keep warm. Stir reserved wine mixture; blend into cooking juices in skillet. Cook and stir over medium heat until thickened and bubbly. Remove from heat; stir in parsley.

Spread each toast slice with one-fourth of the reserved mushroom mixture. Quickly slice each breast half into thin diagonal slices; arrange on mushroom toast. Drizzle about 2 tablespoons wine sauce over each portion.

Sautéed Partridge Breast with Figs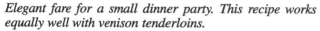

This dish can also be made with ruffed grouse. Serve with buttered new potatoes and fresh asparagus.

- 6 dried figs, chopped
- 1 cup partridge stock (page 145) or chicken broth
- 1 tablespoon butter or margarine
- 4 boneless breast halves from 2 Chukar or Hungarian partridge
- 1 tablespoon balsamic vinegar*
- ¼ teaspoon dried thyme leaves
- ¼ cup butter, cut into 4 pieces
  Salt and freshly ground black pepper

2 servings

In small saucepan, heat figs and stock to boiling. Reduce heat; simmer until the stock thickens and darkens slightly, about 15 minutes. Remove from heat and set aside.

In medium skillet, melt 1 tablespoon butter over medium-low heat. Add breast halves. Cook until well-browned on both sides but still moist in the center, 6 to 10 minutes. Remove from skillet. Set aside and keep warm.

Wipe the skillet out with paper towels. Add the balsamic vinegar; swirl vinegar around skillet. Add the reserved fig mixture. Cook over high heat until the mixture is the consistency of heavy cream. Stir in thyme. Remove skillet from heat. Add butter, 1 tablespoon at a time, stirring well between each addition. Add salt and pepper to taste. Slice the reserved breasts; pour sauce over breasts.

*Balsamic vinegar is a robustly flavored, aged vinegar from Italy. Look for it at Italian specialty stores, or in specialty departments of large supermarkets.

Doves in Corn Bread Stuffing ↑

Moist corn bread stuffing prevents the doves from becoming dry in this classic Southern recipe.

STUFFING:
- ½ cup chopped celery
- ¼ cup sliced green onion
- 2 tablespoons snipped fresh parsley
- ¼ cup butter or margarine
- 3 cups corn bread stuffing mix
- 1 cup upland game bird stock (page 145) or chicken broth
- ½ teaspoon dried marjoram leaves
- ½ teaspoon salt
- ⅛ teaspoon pepper

- 8 dove breasts

4 servings

Heat oven to 350°. Lightly grease 2-quart casserole; set aside. In medium skillet, cook and stir celery, onion, and parsley in butter over medium heat until tender. Add remaining stuffing ingredients. Mix until moistened. Place half of stuffing mixture in prepared casserole. Arrange dove breasts over stuffing. Cover completely with remaining stuffing mixture. Bake, uncovered, until dove is cooked through and tender, about 1 hour.

Quail in Corn Bread Stuffing

Follow recipe above, substituting 6 quail, split in half, for doves. Proceed as directed above.

Hungarian Huns

Buttered spaetzle or kluski noodles, rye bread, and green beans complete this meal.

- 8 slices bacon, cut up
- ¾ cup all-purpose flour
- 1 tablespoon paprika
- 3 or 4 Hungarian partridge
- ¼ cup partridge stock (page 145) or chicken broth
- 3 tablespoons cider vinegar
- 1 small head green cabbage (about 1½ pounds), very coarsely chopped
- 1 medium onion, coarsely chopped
- 1 apple, cored and cut into ½-inch cubes
- ½ teaspoon caraway seed
- ½ teaspoon salt
- ⅛ teaspoon pepper

4 to 6 servings

In Dutch oven, cook bacon over medium heat until crisp, stirring frequently. Remove from heat. Remove bacon with slotted spoon; set aside. Reserve 3 tablespoons bacon fat in Dutch oven.

In large plastic food-storage bag, combine flour and paprika; shake to mix. Add one partridge; shake to coat. Repeat with remaining partridge. Add partridge to bacon fat in Dutch oven; brown on all sides over medium-high heat. Add reserved bacon and remaining ingredients to Dutch oven. Reduce heat; cover. Simmer until juices run clear when thigh is pricked, about 1 hour, rearranging birds and stirring vegetables once or twice.

Stewed Partridge with Sage Dumplings →

STEWED PARTRIDGE:
  3 partridge, whole or cut up
1½ quarts water
  2 bay leaves
  1 teaspoon dried thyme leaves
  1 teaspoon dried rosemary leaves
  1 teaspoon dried summer savory leaves,
     optional
  2 teaspoons salt
 ⅛ teaspoon freshly ground black pepper
  4 carrots, cut into 1-inch chunks
  3 stalks celery, cut into 1-inch chunks
  2 medium onions, cut into wedges

SAGE DUMPLINGS:
1½ cups all-purpose flour
  2 teaspoons baking powder
 ½ teaspoon salt
 ½ to ¾ teaspoon crushed sage
 ⅔ cup milk
  3 tablespoons butter or margarine, melted

4 to 6 servings

In Dutch oven, combine partridge, water, bay leaves, thyme, rosemary, and savory. Heat to boiling. Reduce heat; cover. Simmer for 1½ hours. Add 2 teaspoons salt, the pepper, carrots, celery, and onions; cook until partridge and vegetables are tender, about 45 minutes. Remove from heat. Remove partridge and bay leaves from stock and vegetables; discard bay leaves. Cool partridge slightly.

Skim fat from broth. Remove partridge meat from bones and any skin. Tear meat into bite-size pieces and return to broth. Discard bones and skin.

To make dumplings, in medium mixing bowl, combine flour, baking powder, ½ teaspoon salt, and the sage; stir with fork to combine. Add milk and melted butter; stir until flour is moistened. Set aside.

Heat meat, vegetables, and broth until broth boils. Drop dumpling dough by heaping tablespoons onto broth mixture. Cook over medium-high heat for 5 minutes; cover and cook until dumplings are firm, about 10 minutes longer.

Woodcock in Chablis   VERY FAST

Serve this over toast points or rice as a brunch, light dinner, or hearty post-hunt breakfast.

6 to 8 woodcock breasts and legs, skinned
  3 tablespoons butter or margarine
  1 medium onion, thinly sliced
  1 cup sliced fresh mushrooms
  1 cup upland game bird stock (page 145) or
     chicken broth
 ½ cup chablis or dry white wine
  3 tablespoons all-purpose flour
 ½ teaspoon salt
    Dash pepper

2 to 4 servings

Bone woodcock breasts. Trim and discard any fat from breasts or legs. Discard fat and bones. In medium skillet, melt butter over medium heat. Add woodcock legs and boneless breast halves. Cook until woodcock has just lost its color. Remove woodcock from skillet with slotted spoon. Set aside.

Cook and stir onion in skillet over medium heat for 4 minutes. Add mushrooms. Cook and stir until vegetables are tender, 2 to 3 minutes. Return woodcock to skillet. In small bowl, blend remaining ingredients. Pour over woodcock and vegetables. Heat until bubbly, stirring constantly. Reduce heat; cover. Simmer until woodcock is tender, about 10 minutes, stirring once.

Deep-frying a Whole Wild Turkey

If you've never had a deep-fried whole turkey, you may be in for a surprise. This southern-inspired method produces a bird with deliciously moist meat and crispy skin; the hot oil seals the outside almost immediately, preventing the meat from absorbing oil and becoming greasy.

Many cooks flavor the meat with a marinade or seasoned brine, which is usually injected into the turkey (often a day or two before cooking); others simply season the outside of the bird and let the seasonings permeate a few hours to overnight before cooking. Injection-seasoning adds flavor to the bird, but also may obscure the delicious natural flavor of the wild bird.

Commercial brines and flavorings are available from turkey-fryer manufacturers, as are the special poultry needles used to inject the birds with the seasoned liquid.

Special turkey fryers are very helpful for this technique. Without such a specialty appliance, you need to rig up a very large pot, powerful heat source and a method of getting the turkey into—and out of—boiling-hot fat. Whether you use a special turkey fryer or a homemade setup, plan on cooking the turkey out-of-doors. Spattering oil and fumes would be a problem in an indoor setting. Follow all safety instructions carefully, to avoid an accident with the hot oil.

Deep-fried Wild Turkey

1 dressed wild turkey, preferably skin-on
1¼ cups marinade (purchased, or from the recipe below), optional creole seasoning blend, or other seasoning blend of your choice peanut oil or vegetable oil (approximately 5 gallons)

OO? servings

Follow the step-by-step instructions on the next page.

Easy Creole Marinade

¼ cup crab boil spices, such as Zatarain's
1¼ cups water

OO? servings

Combine crab boil spices and water in small saucepan. Heat to boiling, stirring to blend. Remove from heat and allow to cool completely. Strain out whole spices and reserve, using liquid to inject turkey. Rub reserved spices in cavity of bird after injecting.

Deep-frying a Whole Wild Turkey

1. TURKEY fryers make the task of frying a whole turkey easy. These specialty appliances include a basket or rack that holds the turkey in the hot oil. Most use a propane heat source and are intended for outdoor use. Smaller cookers work well for smaller birds and can also be used to deep-fry fish, onion rings or other foods.

2. PLACE the turkey in the fryer basket, then place into the empty cooking pot. Add cold water to cover the turkey by 1 to 2 inches. Remove the basket and turkey, and note the water level in the pot; this is the amount of oil you should use. You may also measure the water.

3. ADD flavoring to the turkey by injecting it with marinade, using a special meat injector pump. (This step is optional, but it does add flavor and juiciness.) Fill the pump, push the tip into the turkey and gradually depress the plunger while slowly pulling the tip out, until pump is empty. Inject marinade once in each leg, and twice in each thigh and breast, or follow instructions on injector package. You may wrap the injected turkey in plastic and refrigerate it for up to 2 days before cooking, or cook the same day.

4. RUB the outside of the turkey with seasoning mix after patting it dry; sprinkle the inside generously with additional seasoning. If you have injected the bird, rub the seasoning on the bird just before cooking; otherwise, you may want to season the bird and refrigerate it for a few hours (or overnight) to allow the spices to penetrate. Heat the measured amount of oil in the cooker until it reaches 350°F. Place turkey in basket.

5. LOWER the turkey very slowly and carefully into the pot of hot oil. If you add it too quickly, the oil may splash out and burn you. Keep children and pets away from the cooker at all times. Follow all safety precautions indicated in the manual that came with the cooker.

6. COOK turkey for 3½ minutes per pound, then carefully remove turkey and check temperature of thigh meat. It will read 180°F when done. If necessary, return turkey to oil until done. Place cooked turkey on newspapers that have been covered with paper towels, cover with a tent of paper and drain for 15 to 30 minutes before carving.

Blue Goose with Cherries

This recipe can also be used for a large duck, like a canvasback or mallard, or for two smaller ducks.

2 to 3-pound blue goose, skin on or skinned
1 can (16 ounces) pitted dark sweet cherries
1 tablespoon butter or margarine
1 tablespoon vegetable oil
1 small onion, chopped
1 tablespoon all-purpose flour
½ cup water
2 tablespoons cream sherry
1 tablespoon packed brown sugar
1 teaspoon instant beef bouillon granules
½ teaspoon ground cinnamon
¼ teaspoon salt
2 tablespoons cold water, optional
1 to 2 tablespoons cornstarch, optional

2 or 3 servings

Split goose into halves (page 39), removing backbone. Cut each half into two pieces, cutting at a right angle to the first cuts.* Set aside. Drain cherries, reserving ½ cup juice. Set aside. In Dutch oven, melt butter in oil over medium heat. Add onion. Cook and stir until tender. Add goose pieces; brown lightly on all sides. Remove goose pieces; set aside.

Stir flour into onion mixture. Stir in reserved cherry juice, ½ cup water, sherry, brown sugar, bouillon granules, cinnamon, and salt. Add goose pieces and cherries. Heat to boiling. Reduce heat; cover. Simmer until goose pieces are tender, 1½ to 2 hours, turning pieces once. Transfer goose to heated serving platter. Set aside and keep warm. Skim sauce. If sauce is thinner than desired, blend 2 tablespoons water with the cornstarch. Stir into sauce. Cook over medium heat, stirring constantly, until thickened and translucent. Serve sauce over goose pieces.

Variation: Instead of quartering the goose as described above, portion as pictured on page 40.

Blue Goose with Cherries for Crockpot

Follow recipe above, except transfer browned goose pieces to crockpot. Stir flour into onion mixture. Omit ½ cup water. Stir in reserved cherry juice, sherry, brown sugar, bouillon granules, cinnamon, and salt. Cook, stirring constantly, until thickened. Stir in cherries. Pour over goose pieces in crockpot. Cover; cook on low heat until tender, 6 to 7 hours. Transfer goose pieces to heated serving platter. Set aside and keep warm. Skim sauce. If sauce is thinner than desired, blend 2 tablespoons water with cornstarch. Stir into sauce. Increase heat setting to high. Cook, stirring constantly, until thickened and translucent. Serve sauce over goose pieces.

Louisiana Boiled Duck

3 quarts water
1 package (3 ounces) crab and shrimp boil mix*
2 or 3 whole ring-necked ducks or other medium wild ducks, skin on
  Garlic salt
  Pepper
4 or 6 slices bacon, optional

3 to 5 servings

In large Dutch oven or stock pot, heat water to boiling. Add crab and shrimp boil mix. Return to boiling. Boil 5 minutes. Add ducks. Return to boiling. Reduce heat; cover. Simmer until ducks are tender, about 1½ hours.

Heat oven to 350°. Remove ducks from liquid. Drain and pat dry with paper towels. Place ducks, breast-side up, in roasting pan. Sprinkle with garlic salt and pepper. Place two slices bacon across each duck. Bake until ducks and bacon are browned, 15 to 20 minutes.

*TIP: Crab and shrimp boil mix is available in seafood markets, or in the seafood section of large supermarkets.

Duck Breasts with Bacon and Onions

Many people comment that wild ducks, especially diving ducks, taste like liver. This recipe takes advantage of that resemblance.

4 boneless breast halves from 2 wild ducks
½ to 1 cup brandy
¼ cup all-purpose flour
¼ teaspoon salt
⅛ teaspoon pepper
8 slices bacon, cut up
1 medium onion, very coarsely chopped

4 servings

In medium mixing bowl, combine duck breast halves and enough brandy to cover meat. Cover bowl with plastic wrap. Marinate in refrigerator 1 to 2 hours. Drain breast halves; discard brandy. Pat breast halves dry with paper towels. On a sheet of waxed paper, mix flour, salt, and pepper. Dip breast halves in flour, turning to coat. Set aside breast halves. Discard excess flour mixture.

In large skillet, fry bacon over medium heat until crisp. Remove bacon with fork; set aside. Add floured duck breast halves. Fry over medium heat until browned on one side. Turn breast halves over. Add onion. Continue cooking, rearranging breast halves and onions once or twice, until breast halves are desired doneness and onions are tender-crisp. Serve with bacon.

Duck-Breast Rumaki ↑

Duck breast takes the place of chicken livers in this traditional appetizer.

2 boneless breast halves from 1 wild duck
½ cup sake or dry sherry
1 tablespoon soy sauce
1 tablespoon peanut oil
1 teaspoon minced fresh gingerroot, optional
8 to 10 slices bacon, cut in half
16 to 20 canned whole water chestnuts

16 to 20 appetizers

Cut each breast half into 8 to 10 pieces, about 1 inch across each. In small mixing bowl, blend sake, soy sauce, oil, and gingerroot. Add duck pieces; stir to coat. Marinate at room temperature for up to 1 hour. Place one duck chunk and one water chestnut on a piece of bacon. Wrap bacon around duck and water chestnut. Secure with toothpick. Repeat with remaining ingredients. Heat oven to broil and/or 550°. Arrange appetizers on broiler pan. Broil 3 to 4 inches from broiler until bacon is just crisp, about 10 minutes, turning once.

Duck in Corn Bread Stuffing

Follow recipe on page 112 for Doves in Corn Bread Stuffing, except substitute 2 wild duck breasts, skinned, boned, and cut into ¾-inch strips, for doves. Proceed as directed. Bake for 1 hour.

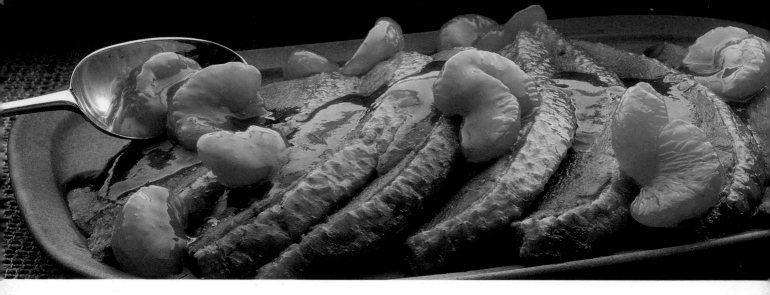

Mandarin Goose ↑

1 whole wild goose, 3 to 6 pounds, skin on
  Salt
1 medium onion, cut in half
1 tablespoon all-purpose flour
½ cup port wine
¼ cup orange juice
1 tablespoon lemon juice
½ teaspoon dry mustard
¼ cup currant jelly
2 tablespoons cornstarch
2 tablespoons cold water
1 can (11 ounces) mandarin orange segments, drained

3 to 6 servings

Heat oven to 350°. Sprinkle cavity and outside of goose lightly with salt; place onion in cavity. Add flour to large or turkey-sized oven cooking bag; shake to distribute. Place bag in roasting pan. In small bowl, blend wine, orange juice, lemon juice, and dry mustard. Add to cooking bag; stir with plastic or wooden spoon to blend into flour. Place goose, breast-side up, in cooking bag. Close cooking bag with provided nylon tie; make six ½-inch slits in top of bag. Roast until almost desired doneness, 15 to 20 minutes per pound. Slit cooking bag down center. Roast until goose is brown, 15 to 20 minutes longer. Remove goose from bag; discard onion. Keep goose warm.

Strain juices from cooking bag into 4-cup measure. Skim fat. Add water if necessary to equal 2 cups. In medium saucepan, combine juices and jelly. Cook over medium heat, stirring constantly, until jelly melts. In small bowl, blend cornstarch and water. Stir into jelly mixture. Cook over medium heat, stirring constantly, until thickened and bubbly. Add mandarin orange segments to gravy; heat through. Serve gravy with goose.

Stuffed Roast Goose

Prepare a young goose with this traditional recipe.

1 whole wild Canada goose, 3 to 5 pounds, skin on
  Salt and pepper
1 recipe Apricot Stuffing (page 142) or other dressing

3 to 5 servings

Heat oven to 400°. Sprinkle cavity of goose lightly with salt and pepper. Stuff lightly with Apricot Stuffing. Tuck wing tips behind back. Tie drumsticks across cavity. Place goose, breast-side up, on rack in roasting pan. Sprinkle lightly with salt and pepper. Roast for 1 hour, basting with pan juices frequently. Drain and discard excess fat during roasting. Reduce oven temperature to 325°. Roast until goose is desired doneness, 1 to 1½ hours longer, basting frequently.

"Poached" Wild Goose

Although this recipe may sound illegal, the title refers to the cooking technique, not the method of procurement! Use this recipe if you have a mature goose to cook.

1 whole wild goose, skin on
1 large onion, quartered
2 stalks celery, cut into 1-inch pieces
2 carrots, cut into 1-inch pieces
1 bay leaf
  Hot water
2 tablespoons butter or margarine, melted

4 to 8 servings

In large stockpot, combine goose, onion, celery, carrots, and bay leaf. Add water to cover. Heat to boiling. Reduce heat. Simmer until tender, 1½ to 2½ hours; if size of goose prohibits covering with water, turn goose over once or twice during cooking. Heat oven to 400°. Drain goose; strain broth and save for other recipes. Pat goose dry. Place in roasting pan. Brush with melted butter. Roast until skin is brown and crisp, 20 to 30 minutes.

Roast Lemon-Mint Duck ↑

1 whole mallard or other large wild duck,
 skin on
1 tablespoon finely chopped fresh mint
 Grated rind and juice from one small lemon
3 tablespoons softened butter, divided
1/4 teaspoon pepper
1/8 teaspoon salt
1 cup duck stock (page 145) or chicken broth
1 1/2 teaspoons finely chopped fresh mint
1 medium lemon, cut into 6 slices

2 servings

Heat oven to 400°. Pat inside and outside of duck dry
with paper towels. In small bowl, combine 1 tablespoon mint, lemon rind and juice, and 1 tablespoon
butter; mix well. Rub butter mixture inside cavity.
Place duck in 9-inch-square baking pan. In small
saucepan, combine remaining 2 tablespoons butter,
the pepper, and salt. Heat over low heat until butter
melts. Brush over outside of duck.

Roast duck until skin is brown and crisp and duck is
desired doneness, 40 to 60 minutes, basting frequently with pan juices. Transfer duck to heated
serving platter. Set aside and keep warm. Pour pan
juices into medium saucepan. Add stock. Cook
over medium heat until reduced by one-half.
Remove from heat. Add 1 1/2 teaspoons mint and
lemon slices. Let stand about 2 minutes. Arrange
lemon slices on duck; pour sauce over lemon slices
and duck.

Grilled Teal FAST

4 whole teal, skin on
1 whole lemon, quartered
 Olive oil
 Salt and pepper
8 whole juniper berries
4 celery tops with leaves
4 small potatoes
4 small white onions
 Dried oregano leaves, optional

4 servings

Start charcoal briquets in grill. Pat cavities and out-
sides of ducks dry with paper towels. Rub each duck
cavity with one lemon quarter, then with olive oil.
Set aside lemon quarters. Sprinkle cavity with salt
and pepper. Inside each cavity, place 2 juniper berries, 1 celery top, 1 potato, and 1 onion. Tie drumsticks across cavity with wet kitchen string. Tuck
wing tips behind back. Rub outside of each duck
with lemon quarter, then with olive oil. Sprinkle
with salt, pepper, and oregano.

When charcoal briquets are covered with ash,
spread them evenly in grill. Place grate above hot
coals. Grill ducks until desired doneness, 15 to 35
minutes, turning once or twice and brushing with
olive oil.

TIP: This recipe also works well on a rotisserie.
Skewer ducks as described in photo sequence on
page 108.

Spicy Duck Stir-Fry with Peanuts ↑

1 large wild duck breast or 2 smaller wild duck breasts, skinned and boned.

MARINADE:
- 1 tablespoon soy sauce
- 1 tablespoon vegetable oil
- 1 tablespoon cornstarch

SAUCE:
- ¼ cup chicken broth or water
- 2 tablespoons soy sauce
- 1 tablespoon sherry
- 2 teaspoons red wine vinegar
- 1 teaspoon cornstarch
- 1 teaspoon sugar
- ½ teaspoon sesame oil

- 2 tablespoons vegetable oil
- 2 tablespoons minced fresh gingerroot
- ¼ to ½ teaspoon crushed red pepper flakes
- ½ cup salted peanuts
- ¼ cup sliced green onions
  Hot cooked rice

2 or 3 servings

Cut duck breast into ¾-inch pieces. In small mixing bowl, blend all marinade ingredients. Add duck pieces. Stir to coat. Refrigerate 30 to 60 minutes.

In small mixing bowl, blend all sauce ingredients. Set aside. In wok or medium skillet, heat 2 tablespoons oil over medium-high heat. Add gingerroot and pepper flakes. Stir-fry about 30 seconds. Add duck mixture. Stir-fry just until duck is firm. Add peanuts. Stir-fry until golden, about 45 seconds. Add sauce and green onions. Stir-fry until thickened and translucent. Serve with hot cooked rice.

Mississippi Duck Gumbo

BROTH:
- 4 or 5 widgeon or other medium wild ducks, skinned or skin on
- 1 medium onion, cut up
- 2 carrots, cut into 2-inch pieces
- ⅓ cup snipped fresh parsley, optional
- 1 bay leaf
- 1 to 2 quarts water

ROUX:
- ¾ cup vegetable oil
- ¾ cup all-purpose flour

- 6 medium onions, finely chopped
- 3 medium green peppers, finely chopped
- 2 cups finely chopped celery
- 3 cloves garlic, minced
- 1 can (28 ounces) whole tomatoes, drained and cut up
- 1 to 2 tablespoons Worcestershire sauce
- 1 tablespoon plus 1½ teaspoons salt
- 1½ to 2 teaspoons pepper
- ½ teaspoon dried oregano leaves
- ½ teaspoon dried thyme leaves
- 1 package (10 ounces) frozen okra cuts
  Hot cooked rice

About 4 quarts

In large stockpot, combine all broth ingredients, adding enough water to cover ducks. Heat to boiling. Reduce heat; cover. Simmer until ducks are tender, 1 to 1½ hours. Remove ducks. Strain and reserve broth; discard vegetables. Remove duck meat from bones. Cut meat into bite-sized pieces; set aside. Discard skin and bones. Skim broth; strain through several layers of cheesecloth. Measure 1 quart broth; set aside. Reserve any remaining broth for use in other recipes.

In large stockpot, heat oil over medium heat. Blend in flour. Cook, stirring constantly, until deep golden brown, about 30 minutes. Carefully stir in onions, green pepper, celery, and garlic. Cook, stirring constantly, until vegetables are tender. Stir in duck meat, reserved broth, and remaining ingredients except okra and rice. Heat just to boiling, stirring occasionally. Reduce heat. Simmer, uncovered, for about 30 minutes, stirring occasionally. Add okra. Stir to break apart. Simmer 30 minutes. Serve over hot cooked rice.

Variation: For easier gumbo, cook ducks in pressure cooker as directed on page 129, or use 4 cups leftover cooked duck, goose, or turkey. Use 1 quart duck stock (page 145) or ready-to-serve chicken broth. Prepare flour-oil roux as described above. Continue as directed.

Mandarin Duck Salad ●VERY FAST ↑

This salad, made with leftover cooked duck, is a lovely blend of tastes, textures, and colors.

2 teaspoons butter or margarine
½ cup sliced almonds

DRESSING:

½ cup olive oil
¼ cup rice wine vinegar or red wine vinegar
1 tablespoon grated onion
¼ teaspoon salt
¼ teaspoon pepper

SALAD:

12 ounces fresh spinach, washed, trimmed, and
    torn into bite-sized pieces
1 cup shredded cooked duck
1 cup sliced fresh mushrooms
1 small red onion, thinly sliced
1 can (11 ounces) Mandarin orange segments,
    drained

4 to 6 servings

In small skillet, melt butter over medium-low heat. Add almonds. Cook until light golden brown, stirring constantly. Remove from heat; cool.

In small bowl, blend all dressing ingredients. Set aside. In medium bowl, combine all salad ingredients and toasted almonds. Just before serving, add dressing to salad; toss gently to coat.

Goose and Wild Rice Casserole

2 cups water
½ cup uncooked wild rice, rinsed
½ teaspoon salt
¼ cup butter or margarine
8 ounces fresh mushrooms, sliced
3 tablespoons all-purpose flour
2 teaspoons instant chicken bouillon granules
½ teaspoon salt
1 can (12 ounces) evaporated milk
⅓ cup water
1½ to 2 cups cut-up cooked goose
1 can (8 ounces) sliced water chestnuts, drained
1 jar (2 ounces) sliced pimiento, drained
½ cup sliced almonds

4 to 6 servings

In medium saucepan, combine 2 cups water, the rice, and ½ teaspoon salt. Heat to boiling, stirring once. Reduce heat; cover. Simmer until rice is just tender, 30 to 45 minutes. Drain; set aside.

Heat oven to 350°. Grease 1½-quart casserole; set aside. In medium skillet, melt butter over medium heat. Add mushrooms. Cook and stir until just tender. Stir in flour, bouillon granules, and ½ teaspoon salt. Blend in milk and ⅓ cup water. Cook, stirring constantly, until thickened and bubbly, about 5 minutes. Remove from heat. Stir in goose, water chestnuts, and pimiento. Pour into prepared casserole. Sprinkle with almonds. Cover. Bake 30 minutes. Remove cover. Bake until casserole is hot and bubbly, 15 to 30 minutes longer.

Preparing Freshwater & Saltwater Fish

The proper care, cleaning and preservation of fresh fish is paramount to ensuring your catch becomes a great-tasting meal. The step-by-step instructions that follow will help you make the most of every fish you put on ice and bring to the fillet board.

You'll find detailed and illustrated instructions on cleaning and caring for your catch, including tips on removing those dreaded Y-bones from northern pike fillets. In the saltwater fish section is a list of substitutions, allowing you to create recipes presented here no matter what kind of fish you have in the freezer.

In the section on cooking methods you'll learn just about everything you need to know to create delicious entrées no matter how you like to cook. From steaming to baking to frying, you'll get insight from our experienced staff who have worked diligently to perfect the recipes. These instructions outline the proper time and temperature to ensure the fish is tender and flavorful every time.

Whether you like a casual shore lunch or a gourmet dining experience, there are recipes for every palette.

Initial Care

Fish are extremely perishable. Fish that do not have red gills, clear eyes and a fresh odor should be discarded. Proper care insures firm flesh for cooking.

The secret to preserving your catch is to keep it alive or cold. If the surface water is cool, a stringer or wire basket can keep some fish species alive. Bring the fish aboard when moving the boat to a new spot. Return them to the water as soon as possible.

Check your catch often, whether the fish are on a stringer, in a wire basket or live well. Transfer dead

WIRE BASKETS or net bags hung over the side of the boat keep small fish alive. The fish should have ample room to move around.

AERATED LIVE WELLS in many boats keep bass, northern pike and other hardy fish alive. Limit the number of fish; remove dead ones to ice immediately.

CLIP-TYPE STRINGERS are preferable to the rope style because fish are not crowded. However, rope stringers are better for very large fish.

ones to an ice-filled cooler immediately. Dead fish left in water spoil rapidly.

Large gamefish should be killed immediately. Use a stout stick and rap the fish across the back of the head. Their flesh can bruise if they flop around in a boat. Field dress (page 8) as soon as possible and place the fish on ice.

Keeping fish in good condition on extended trips is difficult. Fish held longer than 2 days should be super-chilled (page 29), frozen or smoked. You can often take advantage of motel facilities to keep your catch cold or frozen. If shipping fish by plane, place them in a Styrofoam® cooler wrapped with a layer of heavy cardboard.

AVOID placing fish in the sunshine or in a non-porous wrapping such as a plastic bag or rubberized pouch. Fish spoil quickly without air circulation.

COOLERS filled with ice keep fish cold. Crushed ice chills fish faster than a solid block. Drain the cooler often so the catch does not soak in water.

WICKER CREELS are used by wading anglers. Place layers of moss, ferns or grass between the fish to provide ventilation. Transfer to ice as soon as possible.

BURLAP bags, newspapers, moss or materials that "breathe" help preserve fish when ice is not available. Keep the covering moist; evaporation helps cool fish.

Field Dressing

For top quality and flavor, fish should be field dressed as quickly as possible by removing the gills, guts and kidney, all of which spoil fast in a dead fish.

Field dress fish that are to be cooked whole or steaked. It is not necessary to field dress fish if they are to be filleted within an hour or two. Scale fish that are to be cooked with their skin on, but only if they have large scales. These fish include bluegills, perch, crappies, black bass, striped bass, walleyes, northern pike and large salmon.

When field dressing and scaling at home, place your catch on several layers of newspaper to ease cleanup. Before field dressing, wipe the fish with paper towels to remove slime. This makes it easier to hold the fish firmly. If you puncture the guts, wash the body cavity with cold water. Use water sparingly, because it softens the flesh.

The head can be removed after scaling. Paper towels are excellent for wiping off scales and blood spots, and for drying fish.

Field dressing is easier if you have the right tools, and if you clean the fish in a convenient location. Practice the different cleaning techniques until you can clean fish quickly and with little waste.

How to Field Dress Small Trout and Salmon

SLICE the throat connection, the tissue that connects the lower jaw and the gill membrane.

INSERT the knife in the vent; run the blade tip up the stomach to the gills. Try not to puncture the intestines.

PUSH your thumb into the throat; pull gills and guts toward the tail. Scrape out the bloodline with a spoon.

SCALING fish is quick and easy with a scaler, though a dull knife or a spoon can be used. Wet the fish and scrape off the scales, working from tail to head. This job should be done outdoors, because scales fly in all directions. Or, line the kitchen sink with newspapers and scale as carefully as possible.

How to Field Dress Other Fish

REMOVE gills by cutting the throat connection, then along both sides of the arch so the gills pull out easily.

INSERT the knife in the vent. Run the blade tip to the gills. Pull the guts and gills out of the cavity.

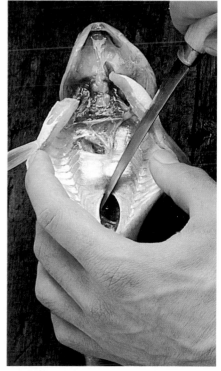

CUT the membrane along the backbone. Scrape out the kidney or bloodline underneath the membrane.

Basic Filleting Technique

Fishermen use a variety of filleting techniques. The method shown below is the easiest and quickest for most anglers. Fillets can be stripped from the backbone in 30 seconds with a very sharp knife. Removing the rib bones takes a few additional seconds. Other methods are described on following pages.

If your fillet board does not have a clip, you can use a fork to pin the head of a small fish. A fork or pliers can also be useful during skinning. Salt on the hands helps hold a slippery fish.

The skin can be removed or left on. Fish such as largemouth bass have strong-tasting skin, so many anglers remove it. However, the skin on small trout and panfish is tasty. Panfish have large scales which must be removed if the skin is retained.

How to Fillet and Skin a Fish

LIFT the pectoral fin. Angle the knife towards the back of the head and cut to the backbone.

TURN the blade parallel to the backbone. Cut towards tail with a sawing motion. Cut fillet off.

REMOVE the rib bones by sliding the blade along the ribs. Turn fish over and remove second fillet.

80

Keep the skin on fillets that will be charcoal grilled. This helps prevent the flesh from falling apart, sticking to the grill and overcooking. Cut long fillets into serving-size pieces before they are cooked or stored. Thick fillets can be divided into two thin fillets for easier cooking.

Remove the thin strip of fatty belly flesh on oily fish such as salmon and large trout. Any contaminants will settle into this fatty tissue. To clean fillets, wipe with paper towels or rinse quickly under cold running water. Dry thoroughly with paper towels.

After filleting, rinse hands with clear water before using soap. Rub hands with vinegar and salt, lemon juice or toothpaste to remove the fishy smell.

Save the bones and head after filleting. These pieces can be used for stock, chowder, fish cakes or other dishes (page 78).

CUT off the strip of fatty belly flesh. Discard guts and belly. Save bones and head for stock.

SKIN the fillet, if desired, by cutting into the tail flesh to the skin. Turn the blade parallel to the skin.

PULL the skin firmly while moving the knife in a sawing action between the skin and the flesh.

Canadian Filleting Technique

Some fishermen find this technique easier than the basic method (page 12), especially when used on fish with a heavy rib structure such as white bass and large black bass. The Canadian technique takes a little longer and leaves more flesh on the bones. But many anglers are comfortable with this method,

How to Fillet Using the Canadian Technique

CUT behind the pectoral fin straight down to the backbone. Angle the cut towards the top of the head.

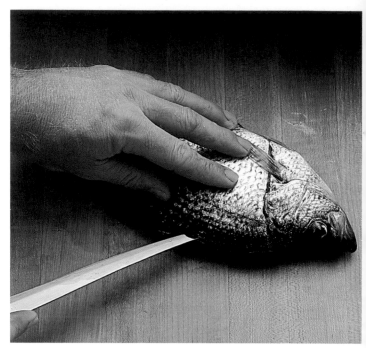

RUN the knife along one side of the backbone. The knife should scrape the rib bones without cutting them.

REMOVE the first boneless fillet by cutting through the skin of the stomach area.

TURN the fish over. Remove the second fillet using the same filleting technique.

because it eliminates the extra step of cutting the rib bones from the fillet. As a bonus, your knife stays sharp longer, because the boneless fillet is removed without cutting through the rib bones. Be careful when cutting the belly, so the knife does not penetrate the guts.

PUSH the knife through the flesh near the vent just behind the rib bones. Cut the fillet free at the tail.

CUT the flesh carefully away from the rib cage. To save flesh, the blade should graze the bones.

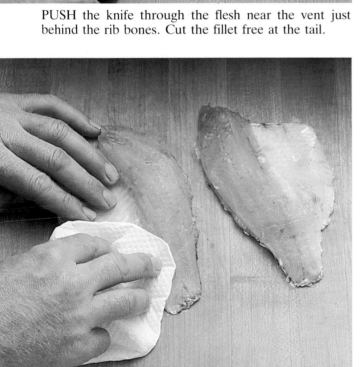

RINSE fillets quickly with cold water or wipe with paper towels. Save head and skeleton for stock (page 26).

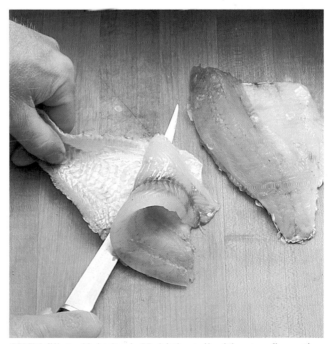

SKIN fillets, if desired. Hold the tail with your fingertips and cut between flesh and skin with a sawing motion.

Filleting With an Electric Knife

An electric knife is particularly useful for filleting panfish, catfish or any large fish that has heavy rib bones. Scale fish before filleting if the skin will be retained for cooking. Skin is usually removed from largemouth bass, striped bass, and other fish which have strong-tasting skin.

How to Fillet With an Electric Knife

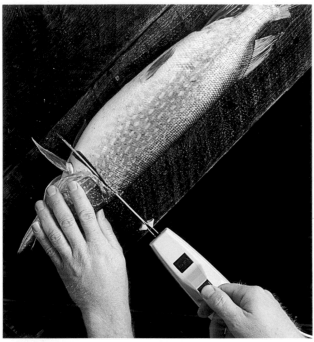

CUT behind the pectoral fin straight down to the backbone, holding the fish at the edge of the counter.

TURN the knife parallel to the backbone and cut toward the tail, firmly grasping the head.

AVOID cutting the fillet from the tail if skin is to be removed. Turn fillet over, hold the tail and begin the cut.

GUIDE the knife between skin and flesh. Remove rib bones with small knife. Turn fish; fillet other side.

Pan Dressing Fish

Panfish, including bluegills, crappies and yellow perch, are often too small for filleting. They are usually pan dressed instead. Scales, fins, guts and head are always removed. The tail is quite tasty and can be left on. Most of the tiny fin bones in a fish are removed by pan dressing.

How to Pan Dress Whole Fish

SLICE along the dorsal fin of the scaled panfish. Make the same cut on the other side, then pull out the fin.

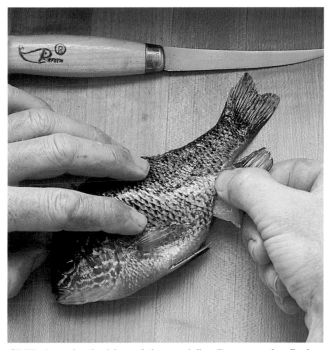

CUT along both sides of the anal fin. Remove the fin by pulling it towards the tail.

REMOVE the head. Angle the blade over the top of the head to save as much flesh as possible.

SLIT the belly and pull out the guts. Cut off tail, if desired. Rinse fish quickly; dry with paper towels.

Y Bones

Northern pike, muskellunge and pickerel have a row of Y-shaped bones that float just above the ribs. The Y bones run lengthwise along the fillet, ending above the vent.

Many anglers remove Y bones before cooking, even though some flesh is lost when they are cut out. The alternative is to pull out the Y bones after cooking.

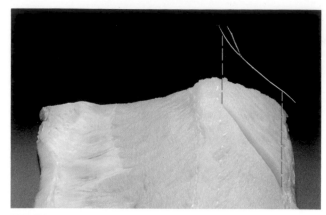

Y BONES lie within a narrow strip of flesh just above the rib cage.

How to Remove Y Bones

SLICE through the flesh along the edge of the Y bones (arrows). The fillet at left will be boneless.

CUT the flesh from the Y bones by guiding the knife blade along the bones (arrow), scraping lightly.

REMOVE the triangular strip of bones and flesh; save them for stock. Two long boneless fillets remain.

Storing Fish

For top flavor, clean and cook your gamefish within 2 hours after catching it. However, most anglers have to keep their catch for a longer time.

The colder the storage temperature, the longer the fish can be held. If handled and cleaned properly, fish can be refrigerated for 24 hours with little flavor loss. Fish stored on crushed ice will remain fresh for 2 or 3 days, but they must be drained often. Super-chilled fish can be kept up to 7 days.

Lean fish can be stored longer than oily fish; whole fish longer than fillets or steaks.

To prepare fish for storing, wipe with paper towels. Rinse in cold water if intestines were penetrated during cleaning.

Super-chilling is storing fish on crushed ice, and covering them with a salt-ice mixture. This method holds fish at about 28°, which is a colder temperature than refrigeration. It is especially helpful on long trips when freezing facilities are not available.

Wrap whole fish, fillets or steaks in aluminum foil or plastic wrap before super-chilling. As the ice melts, add more of the salt-ice mixture.

How to Refrigerate Fish

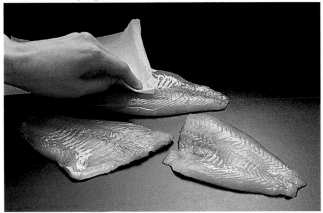

WIPE fillets, steaks or whole fish with paper towels. Or, rinse them quickly with cold water and pat dry.

REFRIGERATE fish on paper towels. Cover them tightly with plastic wrap or aluminum foil.

How to Super-Chill Fish

STIR 1 pound of coarse ice cream salt into 20 pounds of crushed ice to make a salt-ice mixture. If less is needed, cut the ingredients accordingly. Line the cooler with 4 inches of crushed ice. Leave the drain open.

PLACE wrapped fish on the crushed ice. Add a layer of the salt-ice mixture and then more fish. Alternate layers, finishing with a generous topping of salt-ice. Keep the cooler lid tightly closed.

Freezing and Thawing Fish

Freezing is a convenient way to preserve the quality of fish. Freeze them immediately after cleaning unless they will be eaten within 24 hours.

Proper packaging shields the fish from air, which causes freezer burn. Air cannot penetrate ice, so fish frozen in a solid block of ice or with a glaze are well-protected. A double wrap of aluminum foil or plastic wrap and freezer paper is added insurance against air penetration.

Cut fillets into serving-size pieces before freezing. Fish that are being frozen in a block of ice often float to the top before the water freezes. If this happens, add a little ice water and freeze again before double-wrapping. Glazed fish should be checked periodically and the glaze renewed, if necessary.

Store fish in a 0° freezer. If ice cream remains firm, the freezer should be adequate. A frost-free freezer is not recommended, because the fan pulls moisture

How to Freeze Fish in a Block of Ice

SELECT plastic containers, thoroughly washed milk cartons, or small cake or bread pans to freeze whole fish, fillets or steaks.

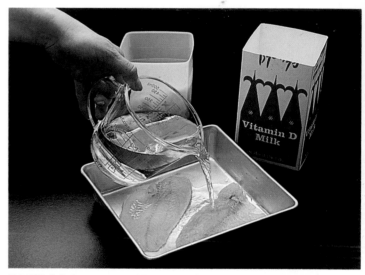

PACK fish for one meal in a container, leaving 1½ inches of airspace; or, layer fish on bottom of pan. Cover fish with very cold water. Freeze the fish in the pan.

Alternate Freezing Techniques

DOUBLE-WRAP whole fish, steaks or fillets that are frozen without a protective block of ice. Separate the fillets or steaks with waxed paper to make thawing easier. This method saves freezer space.

GLAZE whole fish by first freezing without wrapping. Dip frozen fish in very cold water; freeze again. Repeat three to five times, until ⅛ inch of ice builds up. Double-wrap in airtight package, handling fish carefully.

from wrapped fish and quickly causes freezer burn. The chart (right) shows storage times. For top quality, cook within the suggested time.

Fish fillets and steaks may be treated to extend their freezer life by 3 months. Mix 2 tablespoons of ascorbic acid (available in drugstores) and 1 quart water. Place fish in the mixture for 20 seconds. Double-wrap and freeze immediately.

Never thaw fish at room temperature. Bacteria flourishes in warm temperatures. Use the thawing methods described below.

TYPE	WHOLE	STEAKS	FILLETS
Large Oily	2 months	1½ months	1 month
Small Oily	1½ months	1 month	1 month
Large Lean	6 months	4 months	3½ months
Small Lean	4 months	3 months	2½ months

COVER milk carton with aluminum foil. Place lid on plastic container. Freeze. Pop out block of frozen fish from the pan by running cold water on the bottom.

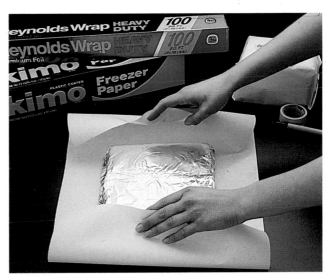

WRAP the solid block of fish in plastic wrap or aluminum foil. Overwrap with freezer paper, sealing tightly. Label package; include species, date and number of servings.

How to Thaw Fish

MELT the block of ice under cold, running water. When fish are free from ice, place them on a plate lined with paper towels. Cover the fish with plastic wrap and thaw in the refrigerator.

THAW ice-free fish by refrigerating them for 24 hours. To speed the process, place the fish in a heavy, *waterproof* plastic bag. Seal the bag, put it in a bowl of cold water and refrigerate. Or, thaw the fish in a microwave (page 59).

← Fish Toast ● VERY FAST

¼ cup all-purpose flour
¼ cup finely chopped almonds
¼ cup water
1 egg
2 tablespoons snipped fresh parsley
1 tablespoon cornstarch
1 teaspoon soy sauce
½ teaspoon salt
½ teaspoon sugar
¼ teaspoon sesame oil
¼ pound walleye or other lean fish fillets
    (page 34), about ½-inch thick
    Vegetable oil
5 slices white bread

20 appetizers

In medium bowl, mix flour, almonds, water, egg, parsley, cornstarch, soy sauce, salt, sugar and oil. Cut fillets into 20 pieces. Stir into flour mixture.

In deep-fat fryer or saucepan, heat vegetable oil (2 to 3 inches) to 375°. Remove crusts from bread; cut each slice into four squares. Top with fish-flour mixture. Fry five squares at a time, turning several times, until golden brown, 2 to 3 minutes. Drain on paper towels. Keep warm in 175° oven.

Salmon Quiche

CRUST:
3 cups all-purpose flour
1 teaspoon salt
⅔ cup vegetable oil
¼ cup plus 2 tablespoons milk

FILLING:
1 cup shredded Monterey Jack cheese
1 to 1½ cups flaked cooked salmon
5 eggs
2 cups half-and-half
¾ teaspoon salt
⅛ teaspoon pepper
    Dash ground nutmeg
2 tablespoons snipped fresh parsley

36 appetizers

Heat oven to 350°. In medium bowl, mix flour, salt, oil and milk lightly with fork until blended. Pat into 13 × 9-inch baking pan, patting dough 1 inch up side of pan. Bake for 8 minutes.

Sprinkle cheese over hot crust, then sprinkle with fish. In small mixing bowl, blend eggs, half-and-half, salt, pepper and nutmeg. Pour over fish. Sprinkle with parsley. Bake until knife inserted in center comes out clean, 30 to 35 minutes. Cool for 10 minutes. Cut into 2 × 1½-inch pieces.

Broiled Bass Canapés ◆ LOW-FAT ● VERY FAST ↑

1 cup flaked cooked bass or other lean fish
   (page 34)
½ cup finely chopped cucumber
2 tablespoons mayonnaise or salad dressing
1 tablespoon dairy sour cream
¼ teaspoon steak sauce
⅛ teaspoon salt
⅛ teaspoon dried dillweed
   Dash pepper
2 drops red pepper sauce
24 to 30 Melba toast rounds or rich round
   crackers
   Sliced pimiento

             24 to 30 appetizers

In small bowl, mix fish, cucumber, mayonnaise,
sour cream, steak sauce, salt, dillweed, pepper and
red pepper sauce. Spread about 1 heaping tea-
spoonful of mixture on each cracker. Place crackers
on baking sheet.

Set oven to broil and/or 550°. Broil 4 inches from
heat until light brown, 3 to 5 minutes. Top each with
pimiento slice before serving.

Broiled Trout Canapés ◆ LOW-FAT ● VERY FAST ↑

1 cup flaked cooked trout or other oily fish
   (page 34)
1 cup shredded Monterey Jack cheese
⅓ cup finely chopped celery
¼ cup dairy sour cream
2 tablespoons finely chopped onion
⅛ teaspoon pepper
30 Melba toast rounds or rich round crackers

             30 appetizers

In small bowl, mix fish, cheese, celery, sour cream,
onion and pepper. Mound about 1½ teaspoonfuls of
mixture on each cracker. Place crackers on baking
sheet. Sprinkle with paprika, if desired.

Set oven to broil and/or 550°. Broil 6 inches from
heat until cheese melts, 2½ to 3½ minutes.

← Garden Salad ⬤ VERY FAST

SALAD:

3 cups torn iceberg lettuce
1 cup flaked cooked panfish or other lean fish
  (page 34)
1 large tomato, cut into 8 wedges
2 hard-cooked eggs, sliced
½ small onion, thinly sliced and separated into
  rings, optional
¼ cup sliced green olives
4 radishes, thinly sliced

DRESSING:

¼ cup vegetable oil
3 tablespoons white vinegar
2 tablespoons catsup
⅛ teaspoon pepper

4 to 6 servings

In medium bowl, combine salad ingredients. In small bowl, blend dressing ingredients. Pour dressing over salad, tossing gently to coat.

Trout Salad With Mustard Dressing

DRESSING:

2 packages (3 ounces each) cream cheese,
  softened
⅓ cup mayonnaise or salad dressing
¼ cup half-and-half
1 tablespoon plus 1 teaspoon prepared mustard
⅛ teaspoon celery salt
⅛ teaspoon curry powder
3 to 4 drops red pepper sauce

SALAD:

2 tablespoons margarine or butter, melted
  Dash garlic salt
½ pound raw shrimp, peeled and deveined
1 bunch romaine
3 cups flaked cooked trout
10 cherry tomatoes, quartered
2 hard-cooked eggs, sliced
1 avocado, peeled and sliced
½ cup sliced black olives

4 to 6 servings

In small bowl, blend cream cheese and mayonnaise. Stir in remaining dressing ingredients. Cover and refrigerate dressing at least 1 hour. In small bowl, mix margarine and garlic salt. Set oven to broil and/or 550°. Place shrimp on broiler pan. Brush with margarine. Broil 4 inches from heat until opaque, 4 to 7 minutes, brushing with remaining margarine once. Turn large shrimp over once.

Arrange romaine on large serving plate. Mound fish in center and arrange shrimp and remaining ingredients around fish. Serve with dressing.

Salmon Salad →

1 cup uncooked small shell macaroni
2 cups flaked cooked salmon
⅓ cup sliced black olives
¼ cup finely chopped green pepper
1 tablespoon grated onion
¼ cup vegetable oil
2 tablespoons red wine vinegar
¼ teaspoon dried oregano leaves
¼ teaspoon salt
⅛ teaspoon pepper

4 to 6 servings

Prepare macaroni as directed on package. Rinse under cold water; drain. In medium bowl, combine macaroni, salmon, olives, green pepper and onion. In small bowl, blend oil, vinegar, oregano, salt and pepper. Pour dressing over salad, tossing to coat. Refrigerate at least 1 hour before serving.

Northern Pike Salad ⬤ VERY FAST

2 cups flaked cooked northern pike or other
   lean fish (page 34)
⅓ cup mayonnaise or salad dressing
¼ cup finely chopped celery
2 tablespoons finely chopped onion
1½ teaspoons prepared mustard
¼ teaspoon salt
⅛ teaspoon pepper

4 to 6 servings

In small bowl, blend all ingredients. Refrigerate at least 30 minutes. Serve on lettuce leaves. Sprinkle with paprika, if desired.

Fish Slaw ◈ LOW-FAT

3 cups coarsely chopped cabbage
1 cup flaked cooked bass or other lean fish
   (page 34)
¼ cup finely chopped carrot
1 tablespoon finely chopped onion
3 tablespoons mayonnaise or salad dressing
2 teaspoons lemon juice
2 teaspoons sugar
½ teaspoon salt
⅛ teaspoon pepper

4 to 6 servings

In medium bowl, combine cabbage, fish, carrot and onion. In small bowl or 1-cup measure, mix mayonnaise, lemon juice, sugar, salt and pepper. Pour dressing over salad, tossing gently to coat. Refrigerate at least 1 hour before serving.

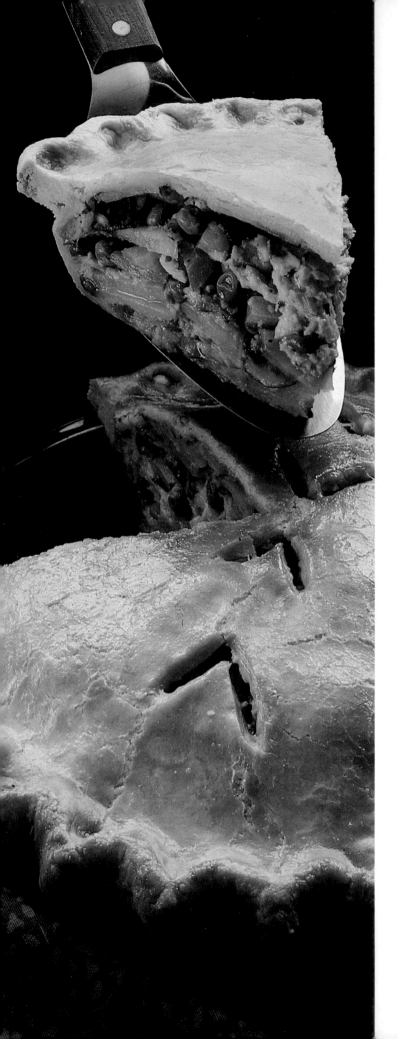

Fish and Vegetable Pie

PASTRY:

  2 cups all-purpose flour
  1 teaspoon salt
⅔ cup shortening
  3 tablespoons margarine or butter,
     room temperature
  5 to 7 tablespoons cold water

FILLING:

  1 tablespoon margarine or butter
  2 tablespoons all-purpose flour
  1 tablespoon snipped fresh parsley
½ teaspoon instant chicken bouillon granules
½ teaspoon salt
⅛ teaspoon pepper
⅛ teaspoon garlic powder
¾ cup milk
  2 medium white potatoes (about 1 pound)
  2 cups flaked cooked trout or other oily fish
     (page 34)
  1 cup sliced fresh mushrooms
½ cup thinly sliced carrot
½ cup frozen peas
  3 tablespoons finely chopped onion
  1 egg
  1 tablespoon water

4 to 6 servings

In medium bowl, combine 2 cups flour and 1 teaspoon salt. Cut shortening and 3 tablespoons margarine into flour until particles resemble coarse crumbs or small peas. Sprinkle with cold water while tossing with fork, until particles are just moist enough to cling together.

Divide pastry in half and shape into two balls. Wrap and refrigerate one ball. On lightly floured board, roll other ball into thin circle at least 2 inches larger than inverted 9-inch pie plate. Fit crust into pie plate, pressing gently against bottom and side. Trim overhang ½ inch from rim. Cover and set aside.

In 1-quart saucepan, melt 1 tablespoon margarine over medium heat. Stir in flour, parsley, bouillon granules, salt, pepper and garlic powder. Blend in milk. Cook, stirring constantly, until thickened and bubbly, about 5 minutes. Set aside.

Heat oven to 375°. Cut potatoes in half lengthwise, then into thin slices. In large bowl, combine potatoes and fish. Add mushrooms, carrot, peas and onion. Stir in sauce.

Fill pastry-lined pie plate with fish mixture. Roll out remaining pastry. Place on filling. Seal and flute edges. Cut several slits in pastry top. Blend egg and 1 tablespoon water. Brush over top before baking. Bake until crust is golden brown, about 1 hour.

Salmon Pie →

CRUST:
  2 cups cooked rice
  3 tablespoons grated Parmesan cheese
  1 egg white
FILLING:
  1 cup flaked cooked salmon or other oily fish
    (page 34)
½ cup half-and-half or milk
  3 eggs, slightly beaten
  1 cup ricotta cheese
¼ cup chopped onion
  2 tablespoons all-purpose flour
  2 tablespoons snipped fresh parsley
⅛ teaspoon salt
⅛ teaspoon pepper
⅛ teaspoon ground oregano
    Paprika, optional

4 to 6 servings

Heat oven to 375°. Grease 9-inch pie plate. In medium bowl, mix rice, Parmesan cheese and egg white. Press into prepared pie plate to form crust. Set aside.

In medium bowl, blend filling ingredients. Pour into rice crust. Sprinkle with paprika. Bake until knife inserted in center comes out clean, 30 to 40 minutes. Let stand 10 minutes before cutting.

Variation: Substitute flaked smoked salmon; omit the salt.

Salmon Loaf With Horseradish Sauce ◇ LOW-FAT

  2 cups flaked cooked salmon or other oily fish
    (page 34)
  2 eggs, slightly beaten
  1 cup milk
½ cup fine dry bread crumbs
  1 tablespoon snipped fresh parsley
  1 tablespoon sliced green onion
½ teaspoon grated lime peel
½ teaspoon salt
⅛ teaspoon pepper
  3 tablespoons prepared horseradish
  1 tablespoon plus 1 teaspoon soy sauce

4 to 6 servings

Heat oven to 350°. Generously grease 8 × 4-inch loaf pan. In medium bowl, combine all ingredients except horseradish and soy sauce. Spread in prepared pan. Bake until center is firm and loaf is golden brown, 55 to 60 minutes. Loosen edges with spatula and turn out of loaf pan; cut into slices.

In small dish, blend horseradish and soy sauce. Serve with salmon loaf.

Baked Walleye and Ratatouille ↑

1 medium onion
2 cloves garlic, minced
¼ cup olive or vegetable oil
1 eggplant (about 1 pound)
3 medium zucchini (about 1 pound)
1 medium green pepper
2 cups sliced fresh mushrooms
1 can (16 ounces) whole tomatoes, drained, cut up
1 teaspoon salt
¾ teaspoon dried basil leaves
½ teaspoon dried oregano leaves
¼ teaspoon pepper
2 to 3-pound drawn walleye

2 to 4 servings

Heat oven to 350°. Cut onion into thin slices and separate into rings. In Dutch oven, cook and stir onion and garlic in olive oil over medium heat until onion is tender, about 5 minutes. Peel eggplant and cut into ¾-inch cubes. Cut zucchini into ¼-inch slices. Core and seed green pepper; cut into ½-inch strips. Stir eggplant, zucchini, green pepper, mushrooms, tomatoes, salt, basil, oregano and pepper into onions. Cook over medium heat, stirring occasionally, for 10 minutes. Set aside.

Place fish on large sheet of heavy-duty aluminum foil. Spoon vegetables over and around fish. Wrap tightly. Place on baking sheet. Bake until fish flakes easily at backbone, about 35 minutes.

Bullheads Marinated in Barbecue Sauce ◇ LOW-FAT

3 tablespoons chopped onion
1 tablespoon olive or vegetable oil
¼ cup packed dark brown sugar
¼ cup catsup
¼ cup cider vinegar
2 tablespoons Worcestershire sauce
½ teaspoon dry mustard
¼ teaspoon salt
¼ teaspoon pepper
⅛ teaspoon dried oregano leaves
1½ to 2 pounds small whole bullheads, heads and skin removed

4 to 6 servings

In small skillet, cook and stir onion in olive oil over medium heat until tender, about 3 minutes. Stir in brown sugar, catsup, vinegar, Worcestershire sauce, dry mustard, salt, pepper and oregano. Cook, stirring occasionally, until bubbly. Reduce heat. Simmer, stirring occasionally, for 10 minutes.

Place fish in medium bowl. Pour marinade over fish; cover. Refrigerate at least 30 minutes, turning fish over once. Set oven to broil and/or 550°. Grease broiler pan. With slotted spoon, remove fish from bowl and place on pan. Baste with marinade. Broil 4 to 5 inches from heat for 8 minutes; turn. Baste with marinade. Broil until fish flakes easily at backbone, about 7 minutes.

Sesame-Dill Broiled Salmon VERY FAST ↑

1 tablespoon sesame seed
1 teaspoon dried dillweed
3 tablespoons margarine or butter
¼ teaspoon salt
⅛ teaspoon pepper
4 salmon steaks, about 1-inch thick

4 servings

Set oven to broil and/or 550°. Grease broiler pan. In small skillet, cook and stir sesame seed and dillweed in margarine over medium heat until sesame seed is light brown, about 4 minutes. Stir in salt and pepper. Remove from heat.

Place fish on broiler pan. Brush with half of sesame seed mixture. Broil 5 to 6 inches from heat for 5 minutes; turn. Brush with remaining sesame seed mixture. Broil until fish flakes easily in center, about 5 minutes.

Sherry Poached Salmon LOW-FAT FAST

2½ quarts hot water
1 cup sherry
1 stalk celery, cut into 1-inch pieces
½ teaspoon dried bouquet garni seasoning
½ teaspoon garlic salt
⅛ teaspoon whole peppercorns
4 salmon steaks, about 1-inch thick
  Sherried White Sauce Variation (page 139)

4 servings

In fish poacher or Dutch oven, combine water, sherry, celery, bouquet garni, garlic salt and peppercorns. Heat to boiling. Reduce heat. Cover and simmer for 15 minutes.

Lower fish into simmering liquid. Fish should be covered; add boiling water as needed. Cover poacher. Simmer until fish flakes easily in center, about 10 minutes. Remove from liquid. Prepare Sherried White Sauce as directed. Spoon over fish.

Fish Creole Salad LOW-FAT FAST ↑

½ cup thinly sliced celery
¼ cup chopped onion
¼ cup chopped green pepper
2 tablespoons margarine or butter
1 can (16 ounces) whole tomatoes
¼ cup white wine
1 teaspoon Worcestershire sauce
1 bay leaf
¼ teaspoon salt
⅛ teaspoon cayenne
   Dash garlic powder
½ pound walleye fillet, about ½-inch thick
5 to 6 cups torn iceberg lettuce

4 to 6 servings

In 10-inch skillet, cook and stir celery, onion and green pepper in margarine over medium heat until tender. Add tomatoes, wine, Worcestershire sauce, bay leaf, salt, cayenne and garlic powder. Heat to boiling. Reduce heat. Simmer, stirring occasionally and breaking up tomatoes, for 10 minutes.

Cut fillet into 1-inch pieces. Stir into tomato mixture. Cook over medium heat, stirring gently, until fish flakes easily, 5 to 7 minutes. Remove bay leaf. Serve over lettuce.

Tossed Spinach Salad

½ pound walleye fillet, about ½-inch thick
MARINADE:
½ cup water
2 green onions, cut into 2-inch pieces
1 teaspoon soy sauce
½ teaspoon salt
¼ teaspoon sesame oil
⅛ teaspoon ground ginger
   Dash garlic powder

SALAD:
½ medium green pepper
2 cups torn fresh spinach
1 cup fresh bean sprouts
½ cup diagonally sliced celery
½ cup sliced fresh mushrooms
4 cherry tomatoes, cut in half

DRESSING:
⅓ cup vegetable oil
¼ cup white wine vinegar
½ teaspoon sugar
½ teaspoon soy sauce
¼ teaspoon salt
⅛ teaspoon sesame oil
   Dash ground ginger
   Dash pepper
1 tablespoon toasted sesame seed, optional

4 to 6 servings

Cut fillet into 1-inch chunks. Place in small bowl. In small saucepan, blend marinade ingredients. Heat to boiling. Pour over fish, stirring to coat. Cover by placing plastic wrap directly on surface of fish. Refrigerate at least 1 hour.

In small skillet, cook fish and marinade over medium heat, stirring gently, until fish flakes easily, 4 to 7 minutes. Remove fish with slotted spoon to paper towel-lined plate. Refrigerate about 30 minutes, until cool. Discard marinade and onions.

Cut green pepper into 2½ × ¼-inch strips. In medium bowl, combine green pepper strips, spinach, bean sprouts, celery, mushrooms and tomatoes. Add fish chunks. In small bowl, blend dressing ingredients. Pour dressing over salad, tossing gently to coat. Serve immediately.

NOTE: To toast sesame seed, cook in small skillet over medium-high heat, stirring constantly, until light brown, 2 to 3 minutes.

Salmon Louis ↑

DRESSING:
½ cup mayonnaise or salad dressing
3 tablespoons catsup
2 tablespoons dairy sour cream
2 tablespoons half-and-half
1 tablespoon chopped green onion
2 teaspoons chopped sweet pickle
1 teaspoon fresh lemon juice
½ teaspoon Worcestershire sauce

SALAD:
4 cups torn iceberg lettuce
2 cups flaked cooked salmon
1 tomato, cut into wedges
1 hard-cooked egg, sliced, optional
¼ cup sliced black olives, optional

4 to 6 servings

In small bowl, blend dressing ingredients. Refrigerate at least 30 minutes. Arrange lettuce in medium bowl or on serving plate. Mound fish in center. Arrange tomato wedges, egg slices and olives around fish. Pour half of dressing over salad. Reserve remaining dressing for serving.

Molded Waldorf Salad

1 to 1½ cups flaked cooked bass or other lean fish
   (page 34)
1 can (8 ounces) crushed pineapple, drained
   and ¼ cup juice reserved
⅔ cup chopped celery
1 medium red apple, cored and chopped
1 envelope unflavored gelatin
1 tablespoon cold water
¾ cup boiling water
1 tablespoon sugar
1 tablespoon lemon juice
1 cup mayonnaise or salad dressing

6 to 8 servings

Lightly oil 4- to 6-cup mold. In medium bowl, combine fish, crushed pineapple, celery and apple. In small bowl, mix gelatin with cold water. Stir in boiling water, mixing until gelatin dissolves. Stir in reserved pineapple juice, sugar and lemon juice, mixing until sugar dissolves. Blend in mayonnaise until smooth. Stir into fish, pineapple, celery and apple. Pour into prepared mold. Refrigerate about 4 hours, until firm.

Unmold onto serving plate lined with lettuce leaves. Garnish with apple slices, if desired.

99

Tomato Baked Walleye Fillets ◇ LOW-FAT ↑

1 medium onion
2 tablespoons olive or vegetable oil
1½ pounds walleye or other lean fish fillets
    (page 34), about ½-inch thick
1½ cups sliced fresh mushrooms
1 can (7½ ounces) whole tomatoes,
    drained, cut up
⅓ cup white wine
½ teaspoon salt
⅛ teaspoon pepper
⅛ teaspoon garlic powder
1 medium tomato, thinly sliced
½ teaspoon dried oregano leaves
2 tablespoons snipped fresh parsley

4 to 6 servings

Cut onion into thin slices and separate into rings. In 9-inch skillet, cook and stir onion in olive oil over medium heat until tender-crisp, about 5 minutes. Set aside.

Heat oven to 350°. Place fish in 13 × 9-inch baking pan. Top with onion rings. Sprinkle mushrooms over onions. Set aside.

In small bowl, combine canned tomatoes, wine, salt, pepper and garlic powder. Spoon evenly over fish and vegetables. Top with tomato slices. Sprinkle oregano and parsley over tomato. Bake until fish flakes easily at thickest part, 25 to 30 minutes.

Herbed Northern Pike and Vegetables ◇ LOW-FAT ● FAST

2 medium zucchini (about ½ pound)
¼ pound fresh broccoli
1 small onion, cut into thin wedges
½ cup thinly sliced celery
¼ cup thinly sliced carrot
2 tablespoons olive or vegetable oil
1½ pounds northern pike or other lean
    fish fillets (page 34), about ½-inch thick
2 tablespoons margarine or butter
¼ teaspoon dried basil leaves
¼ teaspoon salt
⅛ teaspoon dried rosemary leaves
⅛ teaspoon garlic salt
⅛ teaspoon pepper
    Paprika

4 to 6 servings

Cut zucchini into 2 × ½-inch strips. Chop broccoli. In 9-inch skillet, cook and stir zucchini, broccoli, onion, celery and carrot in olive oil over medium heat until tender-crisp, about 10 minutes. Spread evenly on broiler pan. Cut fish into serving-size pieces. Arrange on top of vegetables.

Set oven to broil and/or 550°. In ½-quart saucepan, melt margarine. Stir in basil, salt, rosemary, garlic salt and pepper. Brush on fish.

Broil 5 to 6 inches from heat until fish flakes easily at thickest part, 5 to 8 minutes. Sprinkle with paprika before serving.

Cheesy Northern Pike Bake

- 1 pound fresh broccoli
- 1 pound fresh cauliflower
  (about ½ medium head)
- 1 quart water
- ½ teaspoon salt
- ½ cup thinly sliced carrot
- 2 tablespoons margarine or butter
- 2 tablespoons all-purpose flour
- ½ teaspoon salt
- ⅛ teaspoon dry mustard
- ⅛ teaspoon white pepper
  Dash cayenne
- 1 cup milk
- ¾ cup shredded Cheddar cheese
- 1½ pounds northern pike or other lean fish fillets
  (page 34), about ½-inch thick, skin removed
- 2 tablespoons margarine or butter, melted
- ½ cup fine dry bread crumbs
- ⅛ teaspoon paprika

4 to 6 servings

Cut broccoli stems into ¾-inch thick slices; separate tops into flowerets. Separate cauliflower into flowerets. In 3-quart saucepan, heat water and ½ teaspoon salt to boiling. Add broccoli, cauliflower and carrot; cover. Cook over high heat for 5 minutes. Drain. Rinse under cold running water; drain well. Set aside.

In 1-quart saucepan, melt 2 tablespoons margarine over medium heat. Stir in flour, ½ teaspoon salt, the dry mustard, white pepper and cayenne. Blend in milk. Cook over medium heat, stirring constantly, until thickened and bubbly, about 4 minutes. Stir in cheese until melted. Remove from heat. Set aside.

Heat oven to 325°. Grease 13 × 9-inch baking pan. Place vegetables in pan. Evenly spread half of the cheese sauce over the vegetables. Cut fish into serving-size pieces. Place on vegetables. Evenly spread remaining cheese sauce over fish. Set aside.

In small dish, mix 2 tablespoons melted margarine, the bread crumbs and paprika. Sprinkle over cheese sauce. Bake until fish flakes easily at thickest part, 25 to 30 minutes.

Buttermilk Batter Onion Rings

1 large onion (about 1 pound)
1 cup buttermilk pancake mix
1 cup buttermilk
1 egg
  Vegetable oil

35 to 40 onion rings

Cut onion into ½-inch slices and separate into rings. Spread pancake mix on waxed paper or place in paper bag. In medium bowl, beat buttermilk and egg with fork until smooth. Dip a few onion rings at a time into buttermilk mixture, then coat thoroughly with pancake mix. Let stand on wire rack until dry, 1½ to 2 hours.

In deep-fat fryer or saucepan, heat oil (2 to 3 inches) to 375°. Fry a few rings at a time, turning over one or two times, until golden brown, 1½ to 2 minutes. Drain on paper towels. Keep warm in 175° oven.

Potato Salad

1 quart water
1 teaspoon salt
4 medium red potatoes (about 2 pounds)
3 hard-cooked eggs
½ cup chopped onion
¼ cup shredded carrot
1 stalk celery with leaves, chopped
½ teaspoon salt
⅛ teaspoon pepper
1 cup mayonnaise or salad dressing
1 teaspoon prepared mustard
  Paprika

4 to 6 servings

In 3-quart saucepan, heat water and 1 teaspoon salt to boiling. Add potatoes. Return to boiling. Reduce heat. Cover and simmer until tender, 25 to 35 minutes. Cool. Peel and cut into ¾-inch cubes.

Chop two eggs. Cut remaining egg into slices. In medium bowl, combine potato cubes, chopped eggs, onion, carrot, celery, ½ teaspoon salt and the pepper. Stir in mayonnaise and mustard until just combined. Garnish with sliced egg; sprinkle with paprika. Cover and refrigerate 2 to 3 hours.

Hush Puppies VERY FAST ↑

  Vegetable oil
1 cup yellow cornmeal
⅓ cup all-purpose flour
1 teaspoon sugar
1 teaspoon baking powder
⅛ teaspoon salt
⅛ teaspoon cayenne, optional
1 egg
¼ cup chopped onion
1 can (8 ounces) cream-style corn
2 tablespoons buttermilk

4 to 6 servings

In deep-fat fryer or saucepan, heat oil (2 to 3 inches) to 375°. Mix cornmeal, flour, sugar, baking powder, salt and cayenne. Stir in remaining ingredients until just combined. Drop batter by tablespoonfuls into hot oil. Fry a few at a time, turning over one or two times, until dark golden brown, 4 to 5 minutes. Drain on paper towels. Keep warm in 175° oven.

Vegetables With Crumb Topping 🍅 VERY FAST

Vegetable oil
½ cup all-purpose flour
¼ teaspoon salt
⅛ teaspoon pepper
2 eggs
1 teaspoon milk
1 cup fine dry bread crumbs

RECIPE COATS ONE OF THE FOLLOWING:
1 large onion (about 1 pound), cut into ½-inch
   slices and separated into rings, 35 to 40 pieces
3 medium green peppers, seeded and cut into
   ½-inch rings, about 18 pieces
3 small zucchini (about 1 pound), cut in half
   lengthwise, seeded and cut into
   2½ × ½-inch strips, about 50 pieces
½ pound cheese (Colby, Swiss or Cheddar),
   cut into ¾-inch pieces, about 40 pieces

4 to 6 servings

In deep-fat fryer or saucepan, heat oil (2 to 3 inches) to 375°. In paper or plastic bag, mix flour, salt and pepper. Rinse vegetables (not cheese) with water; do not dry. Shake about one-third of vegetables or cheese in bag until coated with flour. Remove; set aside. Repeat with remaining vegetables or cheese.

In small bowl, beat eggs and milk. Dip flour-coated vegetables in egg, then coat with crumbs. Fry a few pieces at a time, turning over one or two times, until deep golden brown, 1 to 1½ minutes. Drain on paper towels. Keep warm in 175° oven.

Almond Crumb-Baked Tomatoes 🍅 FAST

¼ cup mayonnaise or salad dressing
2 tablespoons dairy sour cream
⅛ to ¼ teaspoon dried dillweed
⅓ cup margarine or butter
½ cup dry seasoned bread crumbs
¼ cup grated Parmesan cheese
¼ cup sliced almonds, chopped
3 medium tomatoes, cut in half

6 servings

In small bowl, mix mayonnaise, sour cream and dillweed. Cover and refrigerate.

Heat oven to 375°. In small saucepan, melt margarine over medium heat. Remove from heat. Stir in bread crumbs, Parmesan cheese and almonds. Place tomato halves, cut side up, on broiler pan. Sprinkle crumb mixture equally on tomato halves. Gently press mixture on top of tomatoes. Bake until base of tomatoes can be pierced easily with fork and crumbs are light brown, 20 to 25 minutes. Serve with mayonnaise topping.

Creamy Northern Pike Casserole

1 cup thinly sliced celery
1 tablespoon margarine or butter
2 cups flaked cooked northern pike or other lean
    fish (page 34)
1 can (10¾ ounces) condensed cream of shrimp
    soup
1 cup frozen green beans
1 can (5.3 ounces) evaporated milk
1 can (4 ounces) sliced mushrooms, drained
1 can (3 ounces) French-fried onion rings, crushed
⅛ teaspoon pepper

4 to 6 servings

Heat oven to 350°. In small skillet, cook and stir celery in margarine over medium heat until tender, about 6 minutes. Set aside.

In 2-quart casserole, mix fish, cream of shrimp soup, green beans, milk, mushrooms, ½ cup of the crushed onion rings and the pepper. Stir in celery.

Bake for 30 minutes. Top with remaining onion rings. Bake until hot and bubbly, 15 to 20 minutes.

Cheesy Bass and Rice Casserole ◆ LOW-FAT

2 cups flaked cooked bass or other lean fish
    (page 34)
⅔ cup uncooked long-grain rice
⅔ cup shredded Cheddar cheese
⅓ cup sliced celery
⅓ cup chopped green pepper
¼ cup chopped onion
1 can (10¾ ounces) condensed chicken broth
1 can (4 ounces) mushroom pieces, drained
1 jar (2 ounces) sliced pimiento, drained
1 tablespoon Worcestershire sauce
¼ teaspoon salt
⅛ teaspoon pepper
½ cup herb-seasoned croutons
⅓ cup shredded Cheddar cheese

6 servings

Heat oven to 350°. In 1½-quart casserole, mix all ingredients except croutons and ⅓ cup cheese. Cover. Bake until rice is tender, 50 to 55 minutes. Stir. Sprinkle with croutons and ⅓ cup cheese. Bake, uncovered, until cheese melts, about 5 minutes.

Smoked Fish Omelet VERY FAST

     3 eggs
     2 tablespoons milk
 1/8 teaspoon pepper
     1 tablespoon margarine or butter
 1/2 cup flaked smoked fish
 1/4 cup shredded Cheddar or Swiss cheese

2 servings

In small bowl, blend eggs, milk and pepper. In 10-inch skillet, melt margarine over medium heat. Pour eggs into skillet. Cook until eggs are set, about 5 minutes. Sprinkle fish and cheese over one half of the omelet. With spatula, carefully fold other half over filling. Cook until cheese melts, 1 to 2 minutes.

Egg Foo Yung ◇ LOW-FAT ● FAST

 3/4 cup water
     1 teaspoon instant chicken bouillon granules
     1 tablespoon plus 1 teaspoon soy sauce
     2 teaspoons sugar
     1 tablespoon cornstarch
     2 tablespoons cold water
     6 eggs
 1 1/2 cups flaked cooked northern pike or other
         lean fish (page 34)
     1 can (16 ounces) bean sprouts, drained
     1 can (4 1/2 ounces) small shrimp,
         rinsed and drained
     1 can (4 ounces) sliced mushrooms, drained
     2 tablespoons thinly sliced green onion
     1 teaspoon soy sauce
 1/8 teaspoon pepper
     1 tablespoon margarine or butter

4 to 6 servings

In 1-quart saucepan, combine 3/4 cup water, bouillon granules, 1 tablespoon plus 1 teaspoon soy sauce and the sugar. Heat to boiling. In small dish, blend cornstarch into 2 tablespoons cold water. Stir into boiling mixture. Return to boiling. Cook, stirring constantly, until thickened and translucent, about 2 minutes. Keep warm over very low heat.

In medium bowl, beat eggs well. Stir in fish, bean sprouts, shrimp, mushrooms, green onion, 1 teaspoon soy sauce and the pepper. In 9-inch skillet, melt margarine over medium heat. Form four patties by dropping 1/3 cup of egg mixture for each patty into skillet. Cook over medium heat for 3 minutes; turn. Cook until set, 2 to 3 minutes. Repeat with remaining egg mixture. Keep warm in 175° oven. Serve warm sauce over patties.

Mushroom Fish Omelet ● FAST ↑

     1 cup sliced fresh mushrooms
     2 tablespoons chopped green pepper
     2 tablespoons chopped onion
     2 tablespoons margarine or butter
     3 eggs
     2 tablespoons milk
 1/8 teaspoon pepper
     1 tablespoon margarine or butter
 1/2 cup flaked smoked fish

2 servings

In 10-inch skillet, cook and stir mushrooms, green pepper and onion in 2 tablespoons margarine over medium heat until tender, about 5 minutes. Remove to small dish; set aside.

In small bowl, blend eggs, milk and pepper. In 10-inch skillet, melt 1 tablespoon margarine over medium heat. Pour eggs into skillet. Cook until eggs are set, about 5 minutes.

Spoon vegetables and fish over one half of the omelet. With spatula, carefully fold other half of omelet over filling. Cook until hot, about 1 minute.

105

Hot and Sour Bass Soup ◆ LOW-FAT

5 cups water
2 tablespoons instant chicken bouillon granules
¼ cup white vinegar
1 medium onion, cut into thin wedges
8 whole peppercorns
¾ pound bass fillets, about ½-inch thick
1 can (4 ounces) sliced mushrooms, drained
1 tablespoon soy sauce
1 clove garlic, minced
¼ to ½ teaspoon dried crushed red pepper
2 tablespoons cornstarch
2 tablespoons cold water
1 egg, beaten
1 green onion, chopped

4 to 6 servings

In Dutch oven, combine 5 cups water, the bouillon granules, vinegar, onion and peppercorns. Heat to boiling. Add fillets. Reduce heat. Cover and simmer until fish flakes easily, about 5 minutes. Remove fish. Cut into 1-inch pieces; set aside. Remove peppercorns. Stir mushrooms, soy sauce, garlic and red pepper into soup. Heat to boiling. Reduce heat. Cover and simmer for 15 minutes.

In small bowl, blend cornstarch into 2 tablespoons water. Stir into soup. Heat to boiling. Cook, stirring constantly, until soup is thickened, about 1 minute. Add fish. Reduce heat and simmer for 1 minute. Remove from heat. Pour beaten egg slowly in thin stream over soup; do not stir. Top with green onion.

Herbed Walleye Soup ◆ LOW-FAT

1 medium onion, cut into thin wedges
1 clove garlic, minced
2 tablespoons margarine or butter
2 cups hot water
1 tablespoon instant chicken bouillon granules
1 cup white wine
¼ teaspoon dried thyme leaves
¼ teaspoon dried basil leaves
¼ teaspoon pepper
⅛ teaspoon dried rosemary leaves
¾ pound walleye fillets, skin on

6 to 8 servings

In 3-quart saucepan, cook and stir onion and garlic in margarine over medium heat until onion is tender, about 7 minutes.

Blend the hot water and bouillon granules into onions. Add remaining ingredients except fish. Heat to boiling. Reduce heat. Cover and simmer, stirring occasionally, for 30 minutes.

Cut fillets into 1-inch pieces; add to soup. Simmer, stirring occasionally, until fish flakes easily, about 10 minutes. Skim fat, if desired.

Fish and Citrus Soup ◆ LOW-FAT

¾ pound panfish fillets
2 tablespoons soy sauce
1 medium onion, chopped
2 cloves garlic, minced
2 tablespoons olive or vegetable oil
2¼ cups water
¼ cup fresh orange juice
¼ cup fresh lemon juice
1½ teaspoons instant chicken bouillon granules
1 teaspoon grated orange rind
1 teaspoon grated lemon rind
1 teaspoon sugar
⅛ teaspoon pepper

4 to 6 servings

Cut fillets into 1-inch pieces. In small bowl, mix fish and soy sauce. Cover and refrigerate at least 1 hour, stirring once to keep fish pieces coated.

In 2-quart saucepan, cook and stir onion and garlic in olive oil over medium heat until tender, about 3 minutes. Add remaining ingredients except fish. Heat to boiling. Reduce heat and simmer for 5 minutes. Add fish and soy sauce. Simmer, stirring gently, until fish flakes easily, about 8 minutes.

Smoked Fish and Potato Casserole  LOW-FAT

4 medium white potatoes (about 2 pounds)
1 medium onion, chopped
1½ cups flaked smoked fish
3 tablespoons margarine or butter
2 tablespoons snipped fresh parsley
¼ teaspoon pepper
⅓ cup water

4 to 6 servings

Heat oven to 350°. Grease 2-quart casserole. Cut potatoes into thin slices. Layer half each of the potato slices, onion, fish, margarine, parsley and pepper in casserole. Repeat layers. Pour water over layers in casserole; cover. Bake until potatoes are tender, about 1¼ hours. Serve with margarine and snipped fresh parsley, if desired.

Trout and Corn Bake

1 medium green pepper
1 tablespoon margarine or butter
4 slices bacon, cut up
1½ cups flaked cooked trout or other oily fish (page 34)
1 package (10 ounces) frozen whole kernel corn
1 cup coarse cracker crumbs
1 can (13 ounces) evaporated milk
3 tablespoons margarine or butter, melted
2 tablespoons grated onion
2 tablespoons snipped fresh parsley
½ teaspoon celery salt
⅛ teaspoon pepper
⅓ cup grated Parmesan cheese
⅛ teaspoon paprika

4 to 6 servings

Heat oven to 350°. Grease 9 × 9-inch baking pan. Core and seed green pepper. Cut two thin rings and set aside. Chop remaining green pepper. In 9-inch skillet, cook and stir chopped green pepper in 1 tablespoon margarine over medium heat until tender-crisp, about 4 minutes. Remove to medium bowl. Set aside.

In 9-inch skillet, cook and stir bacon over medium-high heat until crisp. Remove bacon with slotted spoon. Add bacon and 1 tablespoon bacon fat to green pepper. Discard remaining bacon fat. Stir in fish, corn, cracker crumbs, evaporated milk, melted margarine, onion, parsley, celery salt and pepper. Spread fish mixture in prepared pan.

In small dish, mix Parmesan cheese and paprika. Sprinkle over fish. Top with reserved green pepper rings. Bake until knife inserted in center comes out clean, 40 to 45 minutes. Let stand 5 minutes. Cut into squares to serve.

← Sour Cream Fish Bake

    1 quart water
    1 teaspoon salt
    4 large red potatoes (about 2 pounds)
    6 slices bacon, cut up
1½ pounds northern pike or other lean fish fillets
      (page 34), about ½-inch thick
    1 medium onion
    1 medium green pepper
1½ cups dairy sour cream
    ½ cup half-and-half
    2 teaspoons dried chopped chives
    ½ teaspoon salt
    ⅛ teaspoon pepper
    ¼ cup snipped fresh parsley

6 to 8 servings

In 2-quart saucepan, heat water and 1 teaspoon salt to boiling. Add potatoes. Return to boiling. Reduce heat. Cover and simmer until potatoes are fork tender, about 30 minutes. Drain. Cool and slice.

In small skillet, cook and stir bacon over medium-high heat until brown, but not crisp, about 7 minutes. Drain, reserving 2 tablespoons fat. Set bacon aside. Cut fish into serving-size pieces. Slice onion and separate into rings. Core and seed green pepper; cut into rings. Set aside.

Heat oven to 325°. Grease 13 × 9-inch baking pan. Layer potato slices in pan. Pour reserved bacon fat over potatoes.

In small bowl, blend sour cream, half-and-half, chives, ½ teaspoon salt and the pepper. Spoon one-third of mixture over potatoes. Layer fish and onion rings over sour cream and potatoes. Spoon on remaining sour cream. Top with green pepper rings, parsley and bacon. Bake until fish in center of pan flakes easily, about 1 hour.

Bass With Blue Cheese Sauce

    1 tablespoon all-purpose flour
    1 cup dairy sour cream
   ¾ cup white wine
    2 ounces blue cheese, crumbled
    1 tablespoon dried chopped chives
      Dash white pepper
1½ pounds bass or other lean fish fillets (page 34),
      ¼- to ½-inch thick

4 to 6 servings

Heat oven to 300°. Grease 13 × 9-inch baking pan. In small bowl, mix flour and sour cream. Blend in wine, cheese, chives and white pepper. Cut fish into serving-size pieces. Place in prepared pan. Spread with sauce. Bake until fish flakes easily at thickest part, 30 to 40 minutes. Place fish on warm serving plate. Stir sauce before serving.

Lemon-Cucumber Stuffed Trout →

½ cup chopped, seeded, peeled cucumber
½ cup shredded carrot
 2 tablespoons chopped onion
½ teaspoon lemon pepper
¼ cup margarine or butter
½ cup hot water
 1 teaspoon instant chicken bouillon granules
 2 tablespoons snipped fresh parsley
 3 cups dry bread cubes
 4 small drawn trout, about ½ pound each

4 servings

Heat oven to 375°. Grease 13 × 9-inch baking pan. In small skillet, cook and stir cucumber, carrot, onion and lemon pepper in margarine over medium heat until tender, about 6 minutes. Blend in water and bouillon granules. Heat to boiling. Add parsley. Remove from heat.

In medium bowl, stir bread cubes into vegetables until coated. Place fish in prepared pan. Stuff each trout with one-fourth of bread mixture. If desired, brush fish with 2 tablespoons melted margarine or butter before baking. Bake until fish flakes easily at backbone, about 20 minutes.

Wild Rice Stuffed Trout

 1 cup uncooked wild rice
2½ cups hot water
 1 teaspoon salt
⅓ cup chopped water chestnuts
¼ cup chopped green onions
 1 tablespoon chopped stuffed green olives
 3 tablespoons margarine or butter
 4 small drawn trout, about ½ pound each

4 servings

Rinse and drain rice. In 3-quart saucepan, combine rice, water and salt. Heat to boiling, stirring one or two times. Reduce heat. Cover and simmer until rice is tender, 40 to 50 minutes, checking one or two times to be sure rice is not sticking. Add a few tablespoons water, if necessary. Set aside.

Heat oven to 375°. Grease 13 × 9-inch baking pan. In small skillet, cook and stir water chestnuts, green onions and olives in margarine over medium heat for 2 minutes. Stir into rice.

Place trout in prepared pan. Stuff with wild rice. If desired, brush fish with 2 tablespoons melted margarine or butter before baking. Bake until fish flakes easily at backbone, about 20 minutes.

Creamy Tomato and Panfish Soup ◆LOW-FAT

2 large red potatoes (about 1 pound)
1 medium onion, chopped
¼ cup chopped celery
3 tablespoons margarine or butter
2 cups water
1 can (16 ounces) whole tomatoes, drained
½ cup white wine
1 teaspoon salt
   Dash pepper
3 tablespoons all-purpose flour
¼ cup cold water
½ cup half-and-half
1 pound panfish fillets

4 to 6 servings

Peel potatoes; cut into ¼-inch cubes. Set aside. In 3-quart saucepan, cook and stir onion and celery in margarine over medium heat until tender-crisp, about 5 minutes. Add potato cubes, 2 cups water, the tomatoes, wine, salt and pepper. Blend flour into ¼ cup cold water; stir into vegetable mixture. Heat to boiling. Reduce heat. Cover and simmer, stirring occasionally, until potatoes are tender, 20 minutes. Stir in half-and-half. Cut fillets into 1-inch pieces. Add to soup. Cover and simmer, stirring gently one or two times, until fish flakes easily, about 8 minutes.

← Panfish Chowder

6 slices bacon, cut up
3 medium red potatoes (about 1 pound)
⅔ cup chopped onion
½ cup chopped celery
2 cups fish stock (page 26)*
1 cup sliced fresh mushrooms
½ cup chopped carrot
¼ cup snipped fresh parsley
1 tablespoon fresh lemon or lime juice
1 teaspoon salt
½ teaspoon dried dillweed
⅛ teaspoon dried fennel seed
⅛ teaspoon garlic salt
⅛ teaspoon pepper
1 cup half-and-half
1½ cups cut-up cooked panfish
   (about 1½-inch pieces)

4 to 6 servings

In 3-quart saucepan, cook bacon over medium-high heat, stirring occasionally, until crisp. Remove with slotted spoon; set aside. Peel potatoes and cut into ¾-inch cubes; set aside.

Cook and stir onion and celery in bacon fat over medium-high heat until tender, about 5 minutes. Add bacon, potato cubes, fish stock, mushrooms, carrot, parsley, lemon juice, salt, dillweed, fennel seed, garlic salt and pepper. Heat to boiling. Reduce heat. Cover and simmer until vegetables are tender, 15 to 20 minutes. Blend in half-and-half. Gently stir in fish pieces. Skim fat, if desired.

*Or, substitute 2 cups water and 2 teaspoons instant chicken bouillon granules; omit the 1 teaspoon salt.

Tomato-Dill Fish Soup ◆LOW-FAT ●VERY FAST

3 cups water
1 teaspoon dried dillweed
½ teaspoon salt
   Dash pepper
1 pound muskie or other lean fish fillets
   (page 34), about ½-inch thick
1 can (10¾ ounces) condensed tomato soup
2 tablespoons margarine or butter

4 to 6 servings

In Dutch oven, combine water, dillweed, salt and pepper. Heat to boiling. Add fillets. Reduce heat. Cover and simmer until fish flakes easily, about 5 minutes. Remove fish with slotted spatula.

Add tomato soup and margarine to cooking liquid. Cook over medium heat until bubbly, about 4 minutes. Cut fish into bite-size pieces. Reduce heat. Gently stir fish into soup. Simmer for 2 minutes.

Almond Fried Trout VERY FAST ↑

¼ cup all-purpose flour
⅛ teaspoon pepper
1 egg
3 tablespoons milk
1 cup cracker crumbs
½ cup sliced almonds, coarsely chopped
1½ pounds trout fillets, about ½-inch thick
2 tablespoons margarine or butter
¼ cup plus 1 tablespoon vegetable oil

4 servings

Heat oven to 450°. On plate or waxed paper, mix flour and pepper. In shallow dish or pie plate, blend egg and milk. On another plate or waxed paper, mix cracker crumbs and almonds. Cut fish into serving-size pieces. Coat fish with flour, dip in egg, then coat with almond mixture, pressing lightly.

In 13 × 9-inch baking pan, combine margarine and oil. Place pan in oven for 5 minutes to heat oil. Add fish, turning to coat with oil. Bake 5 minutes. Turn fish. Bake until fish is golden brown and flakes easily at thickest part, about 5 minutes. Drain on paper towels. Serve with lemon wedges, if desired.

Tempura Fried Walleye

1 egg, separated
1 cup very cold water
1 cup all-purpose flour
¼ teaspoon salt
¾ teaspoon sesame oil, optional
    Vegetable oil
1½ pounds walleye or other lean fish fillets
    (page 34), about ½-inch thick
1 cup fresh parsley sprigs, optional

4 to 6 servings

In medium bowl, blend egg yolk and water. Blend in flour, salt and sesame oil until smooth; cover. Refrigerate at least 30 minutes. (Do not refrigerate egg white.) In small bowl, beat egg white until stiff peaks form. Gently fold into chilled batter.

In deep-fat fryer or deep skillet, heat oil (1½ to 3 inches) to 375°. Cut fish into serving-size pieces. Dip fish into chilled batter. Fry a few pieces at a time, turning over one or two times, until light golden brown, about 3 minutes. Drain on paper towels. Keep warm in 175° oven.

With slotted spoon, dip one-fourth of the parsley in the remaining batter. Fry, turning over once, until light golden brown, about 45 seconds. Repeat with remaining parsley. Serve with fish.

← Marinated Salmon Steaks

½ cup vegetable oil
½ cup white wine vinegar
1 teaspoon sugar
1 teaspoon dried parsley flakes
½ teaspoon dried Italian seasoning
¼ teaspoon garlic salt
¼ teaspoon onion powder
⅛ teaspoon paprika
⅛ teaspoon pepper
4 salmon steaks, about 1-inch thick

4 servings

In shallow bowl, blend oil, vinegar, sugar, parsley flakes, Italian seasoning, garlic salt, onion powder, paprika and pepper. Place fish in plastic bag. Pour marinade over fish. Seal bag. Refrigerate 1½ hours, turning bag over two or three times.

Set oven to broil and/or 550°. Grease broiler pan. Remove fish from marinade. Reserve marinade. Arrange fish on broiler pan; baste with marinade. Broil 4 to 5 inches from heat for 5 minutes; turn. Baste with remaining marinade. Broil until fish flakes easily in center, about 5 minutes.

Crunchy Oriental Fillets

½ cup water
⅓ cup teriyaki sauce
½ teaspoon ground ginger
    Dash dry mustard
1 pound panfish or other lean fish fillets
    (page 34), ¼- to ½-inch thick
3 cups chow mein noodles, crushed
¼ cup margarine or butter, melted
½ cup dairy sour cream
2½ teaspoons soy sauce
⅛ teaspoon ground ginger
1 tablespoon finely chopped green onion

2 to 4 servings

In small dish, combine water, teriyaki sauce, ½ teaspoon ginger and the dry mustard. Cut fish into serving-size pieces. Place in plastic bag. Pour marinade over fish. Seal bag. Refrigerate at least 30 minutes, turning bag over one or two times. Drain and discard marinade.

Heat oven to 375°. Grease 13 × 9-inch baking pan. Sprinkle chow mein noodles on plate or waxed paper. Dip fillets in melted margarine. Coat with crushed chow mein noodles, pressing lightly. Place in prepared pan. Bake until fish flakes easily at thickest part, 15 to 20 minutes.

In small dish, blend sour cream, soy sauce and ⅛ teaspoon ginger. Spoon over baked fish. Top with green onion.

Parmesan Bass Fillets 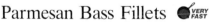 VERY FAST

1½ pounds bass or other lean fish fillets
    (page 34), about ¾-inch thick
¼ cup margarine or butter
½ teaspoon salt
⅛ teaspoon pepper
1 tablespoon fresh lemon juice
1 tablespoon white wine
3 tablespoons grated Parmesan cheese
    Paprika

4 to 6 servings

Heat oven to 450°. Cut fish into serving-size pieces. Place margarine in 13×9-inch baking pan. Place pan in oven for 5 minutes to melt margarine. Place fish in pan, skin side up. Sprinkle with salt and pepper. Bake for 5 minutes; turn. Sprinkle with lemon juice and white wine. Top with Parmesan cheese. Sprinkle with paprika. Bake until fish flakes easily at thickest part, about 5 minutes.

Lemon Fried Panfish

1 cup all-purpose flour
2 teaspoons grated lemon peel
½ teaspoon salt
¼ teaspoon pepper
1 cup water
    Vegetable oil
1½ pounds panfish or other lean fish fillets
    (page 34)
    All-purpose flour

4 to 6 servings

In medium bowl, combine 1 cup flour, the lemon peel, salt and pepper. Blend in water; cover. Refrigerate at least 30 minutes.

In deep-fat fryer or deep skillet, heat oil (1½ to 3 inches) to 375°. Coat fish with flour, then dip in chilled batter. Fry a few pieces at a time, turning occasionally, until light golden brown, about 3 minutes. Drain on paper towels. Keep warm in 175° oven. Repeat with remaining fish.

Saltwater Fish

At one time or another, the cook who wants to prepare fish may face two dilemmas. The first is encountered at the fish market, where the cook, clutching a recipe for halibut, may be disappointed to discover that the price of halibut on that particular day puts it out of reach. Other beautiful and fresh fish is displayed at a more attractive price; what will work as a substitute? The second dilemma is almost the opposite, and is one that I have seen many times in the twenty years I have been teaching fish cookery. In this case, the cook has acquired a beautiful piece of fish—perhaps a less-common species for which there are few recipes available. What now?

Cooking Characteristics

With so much variety in our oceans, it becomes extremely helpful to classify or group fish by certain characteristics. There are three main criteria we need to look at to classify fish. Oil content is perhaps the most important criteria, as it will guide us to the most appropriate cooking methods. Flavor strength is not to be confused with "good" or "bad" quality fish. And texture is critical for proper handling while cooking.

Oil content is key both for nutritional and practical cooking reasons. Generally speaking, the higher a fish's oil or fat content, the higher the percentage of beneficial omega-3 fatty acids. These polyunsaturated oils have been shown to lower triglyceride and cholesterol levels, reducing the risk of heart disease.

From a cooking point of view, the relationship of oil content to cooking method is quite simple: The higher the oil content of the fish, the hotter and more direct the cooking method can be. Leaner fish require more gentle cooking methods, and often need fat added during cooking. For example, very fat fish such as tuna, salmon or mackerel are best with high, direct-heat cooking methods such as pan searing, grilling, broiling or baking with minimal added cooking fat. Lean fish such as halibut, cod or flounder generally need added fat and more delicate cooking methods, such as sautéing, poaching or baking with oil or butter.

The next characteristic to look at is flavor strength. Our oceans supply us with an immense palate of flavors, from robust to delicate. Matching these intrinsic qualities with proper seasoning enhances the natural flavor of the fish; mismatching can destroy it.

Assertively flavored fish such as tuna, bluefish and salmon benefit from cooking with stronger, more acidic ingredients such as red wine, vinegar and mustard, and more assertive flavorings like garlic, rosemary, basil and various peppers. Conversely, milder, more delicate fish such as cod, halibut and flounder need subtler, milder treatment: mild herbs like dill, thyme or chervil and simple preparations such as sautéing with white wine, lemon juice and parsley.

Flavor strength is not to be confused with freshness (or a lack thereof). Any older, less-fresh fish will taste strong or "fishy," but here I am referring to fish that naturally have a full, clearly identifiable flavor. Salmon, for example, has a unique and distinctive taste that most people could easily recognize and identify. Halibut, on the other hand, while equally delicious, is much more delicate and lighter in flavor, and might be mistaken for flounder, cod or other lighter fish.

As always, personal taste should be the ultimate guide when choosing a preparation. I recall a student of mine who loved to fish for halibut. He didn't care for white wine, a common ingredient in halibut recipes, so he perfected a simple halibut sauté featuring red wine, shallots and butter. The moral of the story is that regardless of what any book tells you, the final guide should always be your personal taste.

When we look at a fish's texture we are really asking how firm or flaky a fish is: Is it firm like marlin, swordfish or tuna, or is it flaky like cod, halibut or trout? Firmer fish tend to hold up well to high-heat, direct-cooking methods such as searing, grilling or stir-frying while flakier fish need more delicate treatment such as baking, poaching or sautéing. A chart of some popular fish species follows, ranking their oil content, flavor strength and texture.

SALTWATER SPECIES: COOKING CHARACTERISTICS
Oily Fish

FIRM		FLAKY	
Milder	**Stronger**	**Milder**	**Stronger**
Cobia	Atlantic Salmon	Black Cod	Bluefish
Sturgeon	Barracuda	Chilean Seabass	Mackerel
Swordfish	Bonito		Shad
	King Salmon		Steelhead
	Shad Roe		
	Sockeye Salmon		
	Tuna		
	Yellowtail		

Moderately Oily Fish

FIRM		FLAKY	
Milder	**Stronger**	**Milder**	**Stronger**
Shark	Coho Salmon	Arctic Char	Pompano
	Marlin	Corbina	
		Redfish	
		Spotted Seatrout	
		Tautog	
		Weakfish	

Lean Fish

FIRM		FLAKY	
Milder	**Stronger**	**Milder**	**Stronger**
Grouper	Snook	Atlantic Cod	Lingcod
Monkfish		Flounder	Red Snapper
		Haddock	Rockfish
		Halibut	Sheepshead
		John Dory	
		Orange Roughy	
		Porgy	
		Sand Bass	
		Skate	
		Striped Bass	
		Tripletail	

Saltwater Fish Substitutions

One of the challenges in learning to cook fish is the vast variety of species available. In cooking classes, students often struggle as their purchase or catch doesn't match their selected recipe. What do you do when you have just caught a beautiful seatrout but you can't find any appealing seatrout recipes? Perhaps you have picked out a recipe for baked pompano but your fish store has no pompano that day. Luckily, it is a simple process to learn which fish makes a proper substitution for another fish.

To substitute one fish for another, look at these characteristics, given in order of importance: oil content, flavor strength and texture. For example, if you find a recipe for bluefish, but cannot catch or buy bluefish, look for fish with similar attributes: oily, strong flavored and soft textured. In contrast, a recipe for halibut requires a lean, mild and flaky alternative.

Whenever possible base your seafood choice not on a particular recipe but rather on the quality and value of my available options. If your supermarket has pristine tuna on sale, find a suitable recipe for it rather than purchase an over-the-hill or over-priced swordfish steak. A sterling rockfish fillet will be infinitely more rewarding than a mediocre halibut fillet.

The substitutions below go both ways. If you have a recipe for a particular fish, use this guide to find an appropriate substitute for the fish listed in the recipe; on the other hand, if you have a particular type of fish, look for a recipe that features any of the listed substitutes. This is quite useful to the sport angler, who may find it easier to catch a particular fish than to find a recipe for it.

The listings below cover the most popular saltwater fin fish (although some are anadromous, migrating from fresh to saltwater and back). For a quick overview of possible fish substitutions, also see the chart on page 115.

Arctic char *(Salvelinus alpinus)*

A relative of the salmon; like salmon, char can be freshwater, saltwater or anadromous. Farm-raised and wild-caught. A moderately oily fish with medium-strength flavor and flaky flesh. May be grilled, baked, poached or sautéed. Substitutes: Salmon, trout, steelhead.

Atlantic cod *(Gadus morhua)*

An extremely popular lean, flaky white fish with a very mild flavor. May be baked, sautéed, fried or steamed. Substitutes: Haddock, rockfish, lingcod.

Atlantic cod *(Gadus morhua)*

An extremely popular lean, flaky white fish with a very mild flavor. May be baked, sautéed, fried or steamed. Substitutes: Haddock, rockfish, lingcod.

Atlantic salmon *(Salmo salar)*

Commercially, this is exclusively a farm-raised fish, although many people enjoy fly fishing for these beautiful salmon. The orange to red flesh of this salmon is oily and flaky and yet has a relatively mild flavor. May be baked, grilled, poached, steamed, braised, broiled or sautéed. Substitutes: Any other salmon or steelhead.

Barracuda *(Sphyraena argentea)*

Must be caught in areas away from coral reefs to protect against ciguatera, a potentially dangerous toxin sometimes picked up by reef-feeding fish. Barracuda has delicious grayish blue flesh with a high oil content, firm meat and a medium flavor strength similar to pork tenderloin. May be grilled, baked or sautéed. Substitutes: Marlin, sea trout, cobia.

Black cod *(Anoplopoma fimbria)*

Also known as sablefish or butterfish. Highly prized, extremely oily fish with ivory-colored flesh, buttery sweet and mild flavor, flaky texture. May be baked, grilled, seared, steamed, sautéed or smoked. Substitutes: Tuna, sturgeon, lingcod.

Bluefish *(Pomatomus saltatrix)*

A great sport fish that is also fished commercially. Blueish gray flesh, high oil content, strong flavor and soft texture. May be baked, grilled, smoked or broiled. Substitutes: Mackerel, sea trout, redfish, pompano.

Bonito

Atlantic bonito *(Sarda sarda)*, Pacific bonito *(Sarda chiliensis)*

A small tuna-like fish, usually from 2 to 6 pounds (1 to 3 kg). Flesh is oily and firm, with a medium to strong flavor profile. Bonito may be baked, broiled, grilled or smoked. Substitutes: Tuna, macker

Chinook salmon, see: King salmon

Cobia *(Rachycentron canadum)*

Also known as lemon fish. Caught in the Atlantic and Gulf. Firm, sweet flesh with medium oil content and mild to medium flavor strength. May be baked, broiled, grilled or sautéed. Substitutes: Swordfish, marlin, shark.

Cod, see: Black cod

Coho salmon (Oncorhynchus kisutch)

Also known as silver salmon, these are primarily a wild-caught species although a few are still farm-raised in New Zealand and Canada. Coho is a slightly milder salmon than the sockeye or king salmon, but nonetheless has oily flesh, medium firm flake and a moderately strong salmon flavor. May be baked, grilled, poached, steamed, braised, broiled, smoked or sautéed. Substitutes: Steelhead or any other salmon.

Corbina (Menticirrhus undulatus)

Also known as a white seabass, this relative of the croaker and drum families is a sought-after species both for sport anglers and commercial operations alike. Moderately flaky, with medium oil content and a rich, sweet taste. May be sautéed, baked, broiled, steamed or smoked. Substitutes: Seatrout, redfish, snook, snapper.

Flounder (Limanda ferruginea, Atlantic flounder)

Also known as dab. One of many related flatfish such as fluke and lemon sole. Collectively, these fish are commonly referred to as sole, although the only true sole is the Dover sole from Europe. All of these fish have very mild, soft and flaky flesh and very low oil content. May be steamed, baked, sautéed or fried. Substitutes: Cod, any other flounder, halibut.

Grouper (Epinephelus morio, red grouper)

A family of fish that includes the most commonly seen red grouper. All have mild, sweet and relatively firm but still flaky flesh with low oil content. May be baked, broiled, sautéed, steamed, fried or grilled. Substitutes: Snapper, seabass, any other grouper.

Haddock (Melanogrammus aeglefinus)

These "high-end" members of the cod family have lean, mild-tasting flesh and a flaky texture. May be baked, broiled, steamed, poached, fried or sautéed. Substitutes: Halibut, cod, rockfish, sole.

Halibut

Atlantic halibut (Hippoglossus hippoglossus), Pacific halibut (Hippoglossus stenolepis)

A large flatfish and relative of the flounder family with sweet, flaky white flesh with low oil content. Pacific halibut is primarily caught from Alaska to Northern California. May be baked, fried, sautéed, steamed, poached or carefully grilled. Substitutes: Grouper, cod, haddock, rockfish, seabass, snapper, tautog.el, marlin, cobia.

Chilean Seabass (Dissostichus eleginoides)

Also known as Patagonian toothfish. Not a seabass at all, although it has become known as one. It has jumped in popularity over the last few years and what once was a very inexpensive fish has now become much more expensive. This increased popularity has led to allegations of overfishing. A very mild fish with firm, flaky texture and high oil content. May be baked, grilled, seared, steamed, poached, sautéed or broiled. Substitutes: Black cod, sturgeon, swordfish.

John Dory (Zeus faber)

A famous and world-renowned fish that comes from areas as diverse as New Zealand, the Mediterranean, the British Isles and the Northeast coast of the United States. These fish have a distinguishing thumbprint on their sides, supposedly the mark of St. Peter. Sweet, delicately flavored flesh with flaky texture and low oil content. May be baked, broiled, sautéed, steamed, fried or poached. Substitutes: Sole, flounder, halibut, seabass.

King salmon (Oncorhynchus tshawytscha)

Also known as a chinook, this is the largest member of the salmon family and, along with the sockeye, has the deepest flavor and highest oil content. Kings may be farm-raised although it is usually a wild-caught species. Rich, oily flesh with a firm flakiness and a pronounced flavor. May be baked, grilled, poached, steamed, braised, broiled, smoked or sautéed. Substitutes: Steelhead or any other salmon.

Lingcod (Ophidon elongatus)

A greenling rather than a cod. Highly renowned, especially on the West Coast. Green to white flesh is quite mild but still sweet, with large flaky texture and low to moderately low oil content. May be baked, broiled, grilled, steamed or fried. Substitutes: Halibut, rockfish, snapper, grouper, seabass.

Mackerel, Spanish (Scomberomorus maculatus)

The Spanish mackerel is one of the more common mackerels from a family that includes Atlantic mackerel, cerro mackerel and king mackerel (among many others). All have gray to red flesh with strong, assertive flavor, firmly flaky texture and high oil content. May be smoked, grilled, baked, braised or broiled. Substitutes: Any other mackerel, bluefish, redfish, seatrout, pompano.

Marlin

Blue marlin (Makaira nigricans), Striped marlin (Tetrapturus audax)

These billfish are commercially caught in Hawaii and South America; Hawaiian marlin have more fat and are infinitely better tasting than South American marlin. Marlin has moderate flavor strength, firm texture and moderate to moderately high oil content. May be baked, grilled, stir-fried, braised or smoked. Substitutes: Wahoo, cobia, swordfish, tuna.

Monkfish (*Lophius americanus*)

A strange-looking fish also known as goosefish or angler-fish. Caught primarily for their tail muscles, which have a use monkfish livers. May be stir-fried, sautéed, braised, grilled or poached. Substitutes: Monk is a unique fish and appropriate substitutes are difficult to come by. For certain recipes cobia, scallops or even lobster meat may suffice.

Orange roughy (*Hoplostethus atlanticus*)

Found mostly around New Zealand and Australia, this very mild, flaky, lean fish gained great popularity in the seventies and eighties as an extremely inexpensive alternative to sole, halibut and cod. Roughy became overfished and grew to be quite expensive until recently, when it is neither overfished nor particularly popular. May be baked, sautéed or fried. Substitutes: Cod, sole, halibut, flounder.

Pompano (*Trachinotus carolinus*)

A small member of the jack family that is an absolutely delicious and delicate treat. Rich, oily flesh with moderate firmness and relatively full flavor. May be baked, grilled, steamed or sautéed. Substitutes: Redfish, seatrout, amberjack, yellowtail jack.

Porgy (*Stenotomus chrysops*)

Very similar to Eastern sheepshead (Archosargus probatocephalus). A very common East Coast panfish with mild, flaky flesh and a low oil content. May be sautéed, fried, baked or braised. Substitutes: Snapper, rockfish, seatrout, redfish.

Redfish (*Sciaenops ocellata*)

Also known as red drum. Perhaps the best-tasting member of the drum family. Almost exclusively sport-caught, although it is sometimes farm-raised. This once-plentiful fish fell victim to a huge burst of popularity fueled by the blackened redfish craze (originating with Paul Prudhomme's recipe). It is now illegal to commercially fish for redfish. Nutty, mild flavor when young (stronger as the fish gets large), flaky texture and moderate to high oil content. May be baked, braised, grilled, sautéed, broiled or smoked. Substitutes: Seatrout, snapper, mackerel.

Red snapper, American (*Lutianus campechanus*)

The snapper family consists of about 30 different species including the mangrove, mutton, lane and yellowtail snapper. American red snappers are considered by some to be the best of the snappers, but in my opinion many of the other snappers are equally as desirable. Snapper meat is lean, moderately full flavored with a firm, large flake. May be baked, grilled, steamed, broiled, sautéed or poached. Substitutes: Grouper, seabass, seatrout.

Rockfish (*Sebastes ruberrimus, yelloweye rockfish*)

Yelloweye is perhaps the best-tasting member of the rockfish family. This relative of the perch family is sometimes erroneously referred to as a red snapper. Rockfish has a mild flavor, a large firm flake, and low oil content. May be baked, broiled, grilled, sautéed, fried or steamed. Substitutes: Snapper, grouper, seabass.

Salmon

See listings for individual species: Atlantic salmon, Coho salmon, King salmon, Sockeye salmon.

Sand bass (*Paralabrax maculatofasciatus*)

A smallish saltwater bass found from mid-California to the sea of Cortez, these great sportfish have a mild flavor, flaky flesh and low oil content. May be sautéed, baked, broiled or steamed. Substitutes: Rockfish, striped bass, grouper, porgy.

Seabass

This is an "umbrella" term used to encompass many species including grouper, domestic and European bass, striped bass, black bass and loup de mer. Chilean seabass is technically not a seabass at all; see separate listing. Substitutes: Any of the fish mentioned here will work in a recipe calling for seabass.

Seatrout, see: Spotted seatrout, Weakfish

Shad (*Alosa sapidissima*)

An anadromous species found both in the Atlantic and Pacific, shad spawn in rivers from March to July. Often caught just for the roe, shad is nonetheless a delicious albeit bony fish with a high fat content, soft texture and strong flavor. May be baked, broiled, grilled or smoked. Substitutes: Mackerel, bluefish, seatrout. The roe has no substitute.

Shark

Mako (*Isurus glaucus*), Thresher (*Alopius vulpinus*)

Two of the best tasting and most popular sharks. Firm, moderately flavored flesh with a medium to low fat content. May be baked, grilled, stir-fried, broiled or sautéed. Substitutes: Swordfish, cobia, marlin.

Sheepshead (*Archosargus probatocephalus*)

A member of the porgy family, with very similar characteristics. See porgy listing for cooking and substitution information.

Skate (*Raja binoculata*)

A ray caught in both the Pacific and Atlantic Oceans. This under-appreciated fish has very sweet, mild and lean flesh with a stringy flakiness similar in texture to crabmeat. May be poached, broiled, sautéed or steamed. Substitutes: Scallops or crabmeat work in some recipes.

Snook (Centropomus undecimalis)

This great-tasting fish is exclusively sport-caught. Low to medium oil content, moderately soft flesh, mild flavor. May be baked, broiled, sautéed or steamed. Substitutes: Striped bass, snapper, grouper.

Sockeye salmon (Oncorhynchus nerka)

Sockeye are a slightly smaller salmon (usually from 2 to 10 pounds/1 to 4.5 kg) with a very rich flavor, deep red oily flesh and a firm flake. Sockeyes are always wild-caught, and many people consider a good sockeye to be the pinnacle of fine eating. May be baked, grilled, poached, steamed, braised, broiled, sautéed or smoked. Substitutes: Steelhead or any other salmon.

Sole

This is a term used to describe any flatfish, including flounder, fluke and lemon sole (all of these are actually flounder). Technically, the only true sole is the Dover sole. Substitutes: Flounder, fluke, lemon sole, Dover sole.

Spotted seatrout (Cynoscion nebulosus)

Also called speckled trout. An extremely popular sportfish found primarily from Maryland south into the Gulf of Mexico. Weakfish is also called seatrout, but is a different species; see listing for weakfish. Spotted seatrout has flaky, soft flesh with a moderate to high oil content and a sweet, mild flavor. May be baked, braised, sautéed, broiled, smoked or grilled. Substitutes: Weakfish, yellowtail jack, redfish or red snapper.

Steelhead (Oncorhynchus mykiss)

An ocean-going rainbow trout, steelhead can grow to 25 pounds (10 kg). Delicious rich flesh with a medium flavor profile, high oil content and a medium flake like salmon. Baked, grilled, poached, steamed, braised, broiled or sautéed. Substitutes: Any salmon.

Striped bass (Morone saxatilis)

A popular marine gamefish that is also taken commercially, stripers may range from about 2 to 30 pounds (1 to 14 kg). A hybrid between freshwater striped bass and wild striped bass is also farm-raised (sometimes called "wipers"). Striped bass are flaky and lean to moderately lean with a sweet, mild flavor. Baked, broiled, grilled, sautéed, steamed or poached. Substitutes: Snapper, halibut, snook, grouper.

Sturgeon (Acipenser transmontanus, white sturgeon)

Found in both saltwater and fresh water, sturgeon was once very plentiful but fell victim to overfishing. The harvest has been carefully controlled, and sturgeon is now more readily available both as a commercial and sport-caught fish. Rich, firm, sweet meat with a high oil content. May be baked, grilled, steamed, broiled, sautéed or smoked. Substitutes: Marlin, cobia, swordfish, shark.

Swordfish (Xiphias gladius)

One of the largest members of the billfish family, swordfish have firm, whitish meat with a moderately mild, meaty flavor and a high fat content. May be baked, grilled, sautéed, steamed or smoked. Substitutes: Marlin, tuna, shark, wahoo.

Tautog (Tautoga onitis)

Also known as blackfish. This member of the wrasse family ranges from 1 to about 25 pounds (.4 to 10 kg). Because the primary item in their diet is shellfish, tautog have wonderfully sweet flesh with a low to medium oil content and a firm, flaky texture. Baked, broiled, grilled or sautéed. Substitutes: Striped bass, sheepshead, snapper.

Tripletail (Lobotes surinamensis)

This fish is called tripletail because the tail, anal and dorsal fins are close together and similarly sized. This delicious fish is regularly caught by sport anglers in the Atlantic, Pacific and Indian Oceans; it's also commercially fished. Moderately lean, flaky flesh with a sweet mild flavor. May be sautéed, baked, steamed or broiled. Substitutes: Striped bass, snapper, snook, grouper.

Tuna

Albacore tuna (Thunnus alalunga), Bluefin tuna (Thunnus thynnus), Yellowfin tuna (Thunnus albacaras)

Albacore is a smaller tuna with flesh that ranges from whitish gray to a deep, clear red; it has slightly less oil than other tuna but is still an oily, firm fish with a medium flavor strength. Bluefin tuna has the highest fat content of any tuna and is absolutely delicious; its firm meat is deep red. Yellowfin tuna has a deep red color, relatively strong, meaty flavor, very firm texture and a high oil content. All tuna may be baked, grilled, broiled, sautéed, stir-fried or smoked, and is also prized for sushi. Substitutes: Swordfish, marlin, shark, wahoo.

Weakfish (Cynoscion regalis)

Also known as seatrout, but not to be confused with spotted seatrout (see listing for spotted seatrout). An oily fish with a fine, nutty and sweet flesh and a delicate, flaky texture. May be baked, grilled, steamed or braised. Substitutes: Snapper, redfish or snook.

Yellowtail (Seriola dorsalis)

Also called hamachi or yellowtail jack. These are among the finest-tasting fish in the Pacific Ocean, and command a high price at the sushi market. Moderately strong flavor, high oil content and firm texture. May be baked, grilled, broiled, stir-fried, sautéed, smoked or eaten raw. Substitutes: Wahoo, marlin, cobia.

Asian Steamed Whole Flounder

1 onion, julienned
2 whole dressed, scaled flounder (about 1½ pounds/680 g dressed weight each)
1 bunch green onions, chopped (white parts only)
3 tablespoons (45 ml) soy sauce
3 tablespoons (45 ml) dry sherry
3 tablespoons (45 ml) dark sesame oil
3 tablespoons (45 ml) orange juice
3 tablespoons (45 g) minced fresh gingerroot
2 tablespoons (30 g) minced garlic
½ teaspoon (1 g) ground Szechuan peppercorns

4 servings

Place julienned onion in skillet large enough to hold both fish. Place fish on top of onion, head to tail so they fit snugly in single layer. Whisk together green onions, soy sauce, sherry, sesame oil, orange juice, gingerroot, garlic and Szechuan pepper; pour over fish. Cover skillet tightly and place over high heat. When liquid comes to a boil, reduce heat to low and steam, covered, for 6 minutes, or until fish are cooked through. Serve either whole or filleted, with steaming liquid on top.

Steamed Striper with Scallops and Herbs

2 whole dressed striped bass (1 to 2 pounds/454 to 900 g dressed weight each), boned but intact*
2 tablespoons (6.5 g) snipped fresh dill weed
2 tablespoons (13 g) minced green onions (white and green parts)
2 tablespoons (20 g) minced red bell peppers
½ pound (225 g) sea scallops, thinly sliced
Juice and zest from 1 lemon
2 cups (4.6 dl) white wine or fish stock (page 105)

4 servings

Place bass on steaming rack, opened up and skin side down. Arrange dill, onions, peppers and scallops over opened bass. Sprinkle lemon juice and zest over scallops. Pour wine into bottom of steamer; place rack over steamer and cover tightly. Heat to boiling over high heat; steam until fish and scallops are just cooked through, 8 to 10 minutes. Remove rack; continue cooking liquid until reduced by three-quarters. Pour reduced sauce over fish and serve.

*Have your fishmonger bone out the bass from the inside of the fish, leaving skin and flesh intact while removing the backbone, rib bones and pin bones. If you're handy with a knife and are preparing fish you've caught, you can do this yourself, but it takes some practice, a very sharp fillet knife and a careful hand.

Peppered Tuna Steak

Fresh tuna has a taste and texture that reminds many people of beef, especially when prepared as it is here. I've offered samples of this dish at farmers' markets, and have actually had people argue with me that it couldn't possibly be fish they were eating. A tuna purveyor in Florida told me that after his mother's doctor told her to stop eating red meat, he served grilled tuna to her one evening. Her response? "But I'm not supposed to eat beef anymore!"

4 tuna steaks or other firm, meaty fish steaks, approximately ¾ inch (1.9 cm) thick (6 to 8 ounces/170 to 225 g each)
Coarsely ground black pepper
Kosher salt
1 tablespoon (15 ml) olive oil
½ cup (1.2 dl) dry red wine
2 tablespoons (30 g) minced garlic
1 tablespoon (15 ml) balsamic vinegar
Juice from 1 orange

4 servings

Liberally cover tuna steaks on both sides with pepper and salt, pressing into flesh. In large, heavy skillet, heat oil over high heat until shimmering. Add tuna steaks and sear for 3 to 4 minutes on each side. Remove tuna from skillet, reduce heat to low, and add wine, garlic, vinegar and orange juice, scraping to loosen browned bits. Cook until mixture is thick and syrupy, 3 to 4 minutes. Return tuna to skillet and cook for 1 to 2 minutes, turning once.

Marlin Fajitas

  3 tablespoons (45 ml) olive oil
  2 pounds (900 g) marlin steaks or substitute, cut into strips
     approximately ½ inch (1.25 cm) thick
  1 red bell pepper, cut into 1-inch (2.5 cm) chunks
  1 green bell pepper, cut into 1-inch (2.5 cm) chunks
  1 large onion, cut into 1-inch (2.5 cm) chunks
  4 cloves garlic, minced
  2 teaspoons (5 g) chili powder blend
  1 teaspoon (2 g) cumin
  1 teaspoon (2 g) hot paprika
     Salt and pepper
  1 package (16 ounces/454 g) burrito- or fajita-sized
     flour tortillas, warmed
     Garnishes: Salsa, sour cream, guacamole

4 to 6 servings

Heat large, heavy skillet on high heat. When hot, add oil and heat until shimmering. Add marlin; stir-fry for 3 to 4 minutes. Transfer marlin to plate. Add red and green bell peppers, onion and garlic to hot skillet and sauté until just barely soft, 3 to 4 minutes. Add marlin, chili powder, cumin, paprika, and salt and pepper to taste; sauté for 1 minute longer. Serve in flour tortillas with salsa, sour cream and guacamole.

Baked Lingcod with Apples & Mint Sauce

Lingcod, despite its name, is not a member of the cod family but rather a green-ling. These fish can be caught anywhere from Southern California up through Alaska, and are a highly revered species on the Pacific Coast. The flesh of ling-cod is moderately lean and has a sweet, mild flavor.

  2 pounds (900 g) boneless, skinless lingcod fillet(s),
    approximately ¾ inch (1.9 cm) thick
  ½ cup (1.2 dl) white wine
  2 tart apples, peeled, cored and cut into thick slices

Mint sauce:
  ½ cup (30 g) fresh mint leaves
  ½ cup (30 g) flat-leaf (Italian) parsley
  ¼ cup (53 g) chopped walnuts
  2 shallots, minced
  ½ cup (1.2 dl) olive oil
  1 teaspoon (6 g) salt
  ¼ teaspoon (.5 g) pepper

4 servings

Heat oven to 450°F (230°C). Place fillets in large baking dish. Pour wine over fish; arrange apple slices around edges. In food processor fitted with metal blade, combine all mint-sauce ingredients; process until smooth. With rubber spatula, spread mint sauce over and around the fillets. Bake for approximately 8 minutes, or until just cooked through.

← Seared Shark with Tomato Salsa

Salsa:
  1 jalapeño or other hot pepper
  6 roma tomatoes, finely diced
  3 cloves garlic, minced
    Half of a bunch of cilantro, chopped
  1 tablespoon (15 ml) lemon juice
  1 tablespoon (15 ml) lime juice
  3 tablespoons (45 ml) olive oil
  1½ pounds (680 g) skinless, boneless shark or swordfish steak, cut into 1-inch (2.5 cm) cubes

4 servings

Cut jalapeño in half lengthwise; discard seeds and stem. Mince jalapeño finely; combine in mixing bowl with remaining salsa ingredients. Set aside.

Heat large, heavy skillet over high heat. Add oil and heat until it just begins to smoke. Add shark cubes to skillet; stir-fry for 5 to 6 minutes, or until shark is almost cooked through. Pour salsa into pan, toss very quickly with shark and serve.

Sautéed Weakfish with Bacon, Mushrooms & Onion

Weakfish, also called sea trout, are found from Maine down south to the Carolinas. They have moderately oily flesh and a delicious sweet, nutty flavor. The name weakfish comes from their soft, weak mouths, which tend to rip easily when hooked.

- 3 tablespoons (45 ml) canola or other mild oil
- 2 pounds (900 g) skin-on, scaled weakfish fillets
- ½ cup (70 g) all-purpose flour
- ¼ pound (113 g) sliced bacon, cut into ¼-inch (.6 cm) pieces
- 1 large onion, diced
- ½ pound (225 g) mushrooms, quartered
- 2 tablespoons (30 ml) lemon juice
- 1 tablespoon (2 g) minced fresh rosemary
- 1 teaspoon (6 g) salt
- ½ teaspoon (1 g) pepper

4 servings

In large, heavy skillet, heat oil over medium-high heat. When oil is very hot but not quite smoking, dredge fillets in flour and place in skillet, skinned side up. Cook for 3 minutes per side, or until brown. Carefully transfer fillets to plate; set aside and keep warm.

Reduce heat to medium; add bacon and sauté for 3 minutes. Add onion and mushrooms; sauté for 3 to 4 minutes longer. Add lemon juice, rosemary, salt and pepper. Return browned fillets to pan; reheat fillets for a minute or so. Serve with bacon mixture on top.

Baked Halibut with Saffron Cream Sauce

- 1½ pounds (680 g) halibut fillets
- ½ cup (1.2 dl) white wine
- 2 tablespoons (30 ml) canola or other mild oil
- Salt and pepper
- Saffron cream sauce:
- 4 shallots, minced
- 2 tablespoons (30 g) butter
- ½ cup (1.2 dl) white wine
- 2 teaspoons (.6 g) saffron threads
- 1 cup (2.3 dl) cream
- Salt and white pepper

4 servings

Heat oven to 450°F (230°C). Place halibut fillets in large baking dish. Pour wine and oil over fish; sprinkle with salt and pepper to taste. Bake for 8 to 10 minutes, or until just cooked through.

While halibut is baking, prepare sauce. In medium saucepan, sauté shallots in butter over medium heat until soft. Add wine and saffron; increase heat to high and boil until reduced to ¼ cup (60 ml). Reduce heat to low and whisk in cream, and salt and white pepper to taste. When combined, increase heat to high and cook, stirring constantly, until reduced by one-half. Pour sauce over halibut and serve.

Fish Fillets Baked with Herb Butter

Herb butters are a great way to preserve the flavor of fresh herbs. Whether you grow your own, or buy them at a farmers' market or grocery store, fresh herbs at the peak of their season are a great, convenient way to add flavor to fish. These herb butters freeze beautifully, either simply rolled up in wax paper or put in a tightly sealed plastic container.

- 3 tablespoons (45 g) butter, softened
- 3 tablespoons (8 to 16 g) minced fresh herbs (one or more of the following: dill, chervil, thyme, tarragon, basil, rosemary, marjoram*)
- 2 tablespoons (20 g) minced shallot
- 1 tablespoon (15 ml) lemon juice
- 1½ to 2 pounds (680 to 900 g) mild flaky fish fillets, such cod or haddock

4 servings

Heat oven to 450°F (230°C). In small bowl, stir together butter, herbs, shallot and lemon juice. Arrange fish in an even layer on baking sheet; spread herb butter over fillets. Bake for 6 to 8 minutes, or until fish is cooked through.

*Feel free to substitute herbs in season, or your favorite herb combinations.

Nutrition Chart

If a recipe has a range of servings, the data below applies to the greater number of servings. If the recipe lists a quantity range for an ingredient, the average quantity was used to calculate the nutrition data. If alternate ingredients are listed, the analysis applies to the first ingredient.

	Calories	Fat (g)	Sodium (mg)	Protein (g)	Carbohydrate (g)	Cholesterol (mg)
Almond Fried Trout	623	40.5	406	42	22	153.46
Asian Steamed Whole Flounder	284	12	893	28	12	67
Baked Lingcod with Apples & Mint Sauce	365	23	484	28	9	79
Baked Walleye & Ratatouille	341	16	845	30	23	111.27
Bear Steak Flamade	373	24	410	25	13	30
Bear Stew	348	16	530	29	21	0
Big Game & Onion Casserole Braised in Beer	248	9	380	27	13	105
Big Game Baked Round Steak	292	11	780	34	12	130
Big Game Goulash	302	16	650	17	24	60
Big Game Swiss Steak	249	9	790	28	13	100
Blue Goose with Cherries	798	48	640	47	44	175
Broiled Bass Canapés (1 piece)	34	1	62	2	4	4.86
Bullheads Marinated in Barbecue Sauce	118	4	297	7	14	21.92
Cheesy Bass & Rice Casserole	264	10	694	21	22	61.47
Creamy Northern Pike Casserole	251	14	621	15	15	38.9
Creamy Tomato & Panfish Soup	242	9	645	18	22	75.5
Crunchy Oriental Fillets	468	29	1493	27	25	114.8
Duck with Orange Sauce	670	49	680	30	27	140
Egg Foo Yung	180	7.5	661	21	6	266.99
Elk Tenderloin Saute	289	11	1150	30	16	75
Fillet of Venison (5.25 oz.)	227	9	105	35	0	135
Fish & Citrus Soup	120	5	639	12	6	51.07
Fish Fillets Baked with Herb Butter	299	13	197	42	1	87
Fish Slaw	101	6.5	262	6	4	24.61
Fish Toast (1 piece)	62	3.5	116	2	5	15.56
Garlic Sausage (4 oz.)	181	11	640	19	0.4	70
Goose and Wild Rice Casserole	385	22	920	21	26	80
Grilled Bacon-Wrapped Big Game	207	8	200	32	0.1	115
Grilled Loin with Brown Sugar Baste	233	7	440	34	5	135
Grilled Marinated Pheasants	788	47	160	83	2	260
Hasenpfeffer	454	25	680	41	14	170
Herbed Walleye Soup	79	3.5	447	8	3	36.6
Hot & Sour Bass Soup	116	3	1307	12	8	74
Lemon-Cucumber Stuffed Trout	353	17	651	30	18	76.64
Mandarin Duck Salad	316	26	160	9	14	25

*Dietary Exchanges: S=Starch Fr=Fruit C=Carb/Other V=Vegetable M=Milk(whole) F=Fat VLM=Very Lean Meat LM=Lean Meat MFM=Medium-Fat Meat HFM=High-Fat Meat

	Calories	Fat (g)	Sodium (mg)	Protein (g)	Carbohydrate (g)	Cholesterol (mg)
Mandarin Goose	596	36	125	41	26	150
Marinated Salmon Steaks (6oz. Steak)	463	36.5	157	30	2	82.32
Marlin Fajitas	497	18	494	34	48	53
Mexican Chorizo Sausage (4 oz.)	209	12	500	23	1	90
Mississippi Duck Gumbo	219	13	800	10	17	30
Mushroom Fish Omelet	327	25.5	666	19	5	332.57
Northern Pike Salad	143	10	208	12	0.9	30.71
Old-Fashioned Venison Stew	350	9	490	35	30	120
Panfish Chowder	293	18.5	767	14	18	70.82
Peppered Antelope Roast (4 oz.)	208	10	150	27	0.1	115
Peppered Tuna Steak	304	12	72	42	4	67
Poached Wild Goose	589	43	150	48	0	175
Potato Sausage (4 oz.)	156	6	480	13	11	60
Roast Big Game Tenderloin (4 oz.)	143	6	160	16	5	45
Roast Boneless Sirloin Tip (4 oz.)	159	5	60	26	0	100
Roast Pheasant with Sauerkraut	760	52	1400	59	5	235
Salmon Salad	244	13.5	189	15	14	23.15
Sauteed Partridge Breast with Figs	824	51	890	55	38	240
Sauteed Weakfish w/ Bacon, Mushrooms, Onion	371	23	601	27	13	126
Seared Shark with Tomato Salsa	331	18	143	37	4	87
Sharptail on Mushroom Toast	503	32	610	30	20	125
Sherried Squirrel or Rabbit	385	16	1280	47	9	185
Smoked Fish & Potato Casserole	226	7	438	12	30	11.69
Smoked Fish Omelet	268	18.5	618	22	2	347.45
Southern Fried Squirrel or Rabbit with Gravy	567	29	660	51	22	190
Spanish Rabbit	736	26	1770	55	70	170
Spicy Duck Stir-Fry with Peanuts	477	32	1390	33	14	100
Spicy Elk Kabobs	161	3.5	280	27	4	60
Steamed Striper with Scallops and Herbs	201	4	199	36	4	136
Stuffed Roast Goose	837	43	520	48	56	165
Tempura Fried Walleye	254	9	164	25	16	133.02
Texas-Style Venison Chili	196	6	340	19	17	65
Tomato-Dill Fish Soup	136	5	620	15	7	29.51
Tomato-Rabbit Casserole	571	14	1050	54	57	180
Trout & Corn Bake	421	27	566	20	26	59.25
Tuscan hare with Pasta	364	16	1110	39	16	135
Venison and Beans	376	18	880	21	36	70
Venison Breakfast Sausage (4 oz.)	250	18	520	20	0.2	85
Venison Meatloaf Supreme	362	25	490	24	8	155
Venison Stroganoff	303	16	540	26	11	115
Wild Rice Stuffed Trout	393	14	775	34	33	76.34
Wine-Braised Duck	483	38	420	21	14	90
Zesty Venison Stew	301	8	790	30	28	95

**Sodium content will vary with time in solution.

Index

Creative Publishing international
Your Complete Source of How-to Information for the Outdoors

Hunting Books
- Advanced Turkey Hunting
- Advanced Whitetail Hunting
- Bowhunting Equipment & Skills
- Bowhunter's Guide to Accurate Shooting
- The Complete Guide to Hunting
- Dog Training
- Elk Hunting
- How to Think Like a Survivor
- Hunting Record-Book Bucks
- Mule Deer Hunting
- Muzzleloading
- Outdoor Guide to Using Your GPS
- Pronghorn Hunting
- Waterfowl Hunting
- Whitetail Hunting
- Whitetail Techniques & Tactics
- Wild Turkey

Fishing Books
- Advanced Bass Fishing
- The Art of Freshwater Fishing
- The Complete Guide to Freshwater Fishing
- Fishing for Catfish

- Fishing Rivers & Streams
- Fishing Tips & Tricks
- Fishing with Artificial Lures
- Inshore Salt Water Fishing
- Kids Gone Campin'
- Kids Gone Fishin'
- Largemouth Bass
- Live Bait Fishing
- Modern Methods of Ice Fishing
- Northern Pike & Muskie
- Offshore Salt Water Fishing
- Panfish
- Salt Water Fishing Tactics
- Smallmouth Bass
- Striped Bass Fishing: Salt Water Strategies
- Successful Walleye Fishing
- Trout
- Ultralight Fishing

Fly Fishing Books
- The Art of Fly Tying
- The Art of Fly Tying – CD ROM
- Complete Photo Guide to Fly Fishing
- Complete Photo Guide to Fly Tying

- Fishing Dry Flies
- Fishing Nymphs, Wet Flies & Streamers
- Fly-Fishing Equipment & Skills
- Fly Fishing for Beginners
- Fly Fishing for Trout in Streams
- Fly-Tying Techniques & Patterns

Cookbooks
- All-Time Favorite Game Bird Recipes
- America's Favorite Fish Recipes
- America's Favorite Wild Game Recipes
- Backyard Grilling
- Cooking Wild in Kate's Camp
- Cooking Wild in Kate's Kitchen
- Dressing & Cooking Wild Game
- The New Cleaning & Cooking Fish
- Preparing Fish & Wild Game
- The Saltwater Cookbook
- Venison Cookery
- The Wild Butcher

To purchase these or other Creative Publishing international titles,
contact your local bookseller, or visit our website at
www.creativepub.com

The Complete
FLY FISHERMAN™